Bridge Builders of Nauck/Green Valley
Past and Present

by

Dr. Alfred O. Taylor Jr.

DORRANCE
PUBLISHING CO
EST. 1920
PITTSBURGH, PENNSYLVANIA 15238

Dorrance Publishing Co
585 Alpha Drive
Suite 103
Pittsburgh, PA 15238
Visit our website at *www.dorrancebookstore.com*

ISBN: 978-1-4809-1134-5
eISBN: 978-1-4809-1456-8

Contents

Nauck/Green Valley Bridge Builders

The following are stories, interviews, and biographies of bridge builders (both past and present) who have made local and national contributions and their connections with Arlington County's oldest African American community (1844).

The Bridge Builder

An old man, going a lone highway,
Came, at the evening, cold and gray,
To a chasm, vast and deep and wide,
Through which was flowing a sullen tide.

The old man crossed in the twilight dim;
The sullen stream had no fear for him;
But he turned when safe on the other side,
And built a bridge to span the tide.

"Old man," said a fellow pilgrim near,
"You are wasting strength with building here;
Your journey will end with the ending day;
You never again will pass this way;
You've crossed the chasm, deep and wide-
Why build you this bridge at the evening tide?"

The builder lifted his old gray head,
"Good friend, in the path I have come," he said.
"There followeth after me today,
A youth, whose feet must pass this way.

This chasm, that has been naught to me,
To that fair-haired youth may a pitfall be.
He, too, must cross in the twilight dim;
Good friend, I am building this bridge for him."

By Will Allen Dromgoole

Acknowledgements

No work of this nature would be possible, of course, but for the assistance of many people. Among those to whom I am indebted are the following persons who so willingly served on my advisory committee and provided assistance and the encouragement that enabled this project to get underway effectively. Their assistance in the identification and evaluation of the material of the individuals featured is appreciated.

Thanks to: Dr. Nancy Perry; Ms. Jacqueline Coachman; the late Ms. Joan E. Cooper; Mr. Milton I. Rowe, Sr.; Reverend Richard O. Green, Sr.; Ms. Yolanda Johnson Black; Mrs. Portia Clark; the late Dr. Talmadge Williams; Ms. Katherine Glennon; Dr. Leonard L. Hamlin, Sr.; and Mr. John Richardson.

I am also indebted to my grandsons, Kourtnay M. Taylor and Aaron J. Steele, for their valuable assistance with my IT endeavors.

Throughout this undertaking, my wife, Delores, has been indispensable, not only for her ideas, proofing, and other support and encouragement, but also for her patience in going along with me radically changing our daily retirement regimen to pursue publishing this book and dedicate it in memory of my parents, Alfred and Ruby, and also my sister, Audrey A. Coachman.

Special thanks go out to Mr. David Bearinger, Director of Grants and Community Programs for the Virginia Foundation for the Humanities for his encouragement and belief that this project was worthy of undertaking and its partial funding of its publication.

Alfred O. Taylor, Jr., Ed.D.
Arlington, Virginia
2013

Preface

The Nauck community is a roughly triangular area lying to the south of Columbia Pike and north of Shirlington, bound on South 16th Road to the north, Walter Reed Drive to the west, and Four Mile Run to the south, and it straddles Glebe Road to the east where the Army-Navy Country Club forms its eastern extremity. It is recognized as one of Arlington County's oldest African American neighborhoods, tracing its existence to 1844 when Sarah and Levi Jones established their home. Over the years, many residents labored and contributed to its growth, despite the laws of Virginia that often denied them access to the educational, financial, land purchasing opportunities, etc. to enable them to compete on level ground.

Despite these obstacles, many of its residents persevered to provide those needed services and fought for the right to experience a good quality of life. It has motivated me to compile stories about these pioneers, both past and present, in hopes that their memories will not be forgotten but used as a springboard for instilling perseverance in future generations.

My memories date back to my father, Alfred O. Taylor, Sr., who was always sitting me down and dwelling in me the history of Arlington County from his perspective as one who worked forty-four years for its government. Those stories dwelled mostly on the who's and why's things were or were not happening. The contributions of these ordinary men and women are often unseen as springboards that will propel future generations to exceed their goals and aspirations. Ordinary Nauck/Green Valley residents surviving Jim Crow Laws, lacking financial backing becoming economically independent, educating themselves and their children, fighting for freedom, and remembering from whence they came should be an inspiration to all to celebrate and continue sharing future, ordinary resident's accomplishments.

It is our hope that this document will become a living document that is continuously added to as future generations of "Nauckians" make their contributions to society. This goal is perhaps best expressed by the Akan symbol of the "Sankofa," a mythical bird that flies forward with its head turned backwards. The Akan word "Sankofa" informs us that we must go back and reclaim our past so we can understand why and how we came to be who we are today.

Today the Nauck community is recognized as being one of Arlington County's finest. It is my estimation that the poem, "The Bridge Builder," by Will Allen Dromgoole exemplifies the spirit of these bridge builders/pioneers (both past and present) who labored to sustain the Nauck community to where it is today. The poem continues to be quoted frequently, usually in a religious context or in writings stressing a moral lesson. "The Bridge Builder" is also used to promote the idea of building links for the future and passing the torch along for the next generation. This is the context the author wishes for, in spurring future students, residents, or other interested parties to build on and continue the spirit of these "Bridge Builders."

Alfred O. Taylor, Jr., Ed.D.

Sarah and Levi Jones:
The Original Nauck/Green Valley Bridge Builders

Levi and Sarah Jones House built 1844, no longer standing.

The Jones family traced its roots at Mount Vernon to two of Washington's former slaves, Davy and Evy (sometimes spelled Eby), who acquired their freedom in 1801, along with their two daughters, six-year-old Sarah and one-year-old Nancy. The family eventually grew to include three sons: David, Joseph, and Levi. When the children registered with Fairfax County in 1831, they referenced Davy and Evy in their individual claims to free status (Donald Sweig, *Registrations of Free Negrow*, *Book 2*, pages 66, 96, and 98).

Apparently dissatisfied with the opportunities (or lack thereof) in rural Fairfax, Levi Jones migrated to Alexandria by the early 1840s. Soon thereafter he became a property owner, acquiring fourteen acres of land in 1844 with a down payment of $200 and an additional $235 to be paid over a period of five years. By the time the Civil War commenced, Jones' farm consisted of seventeen acres, twelve of which had been cleared for cultivation. Jones' property eventually became the southern extension of the Nauck community (the location of the Macedonia Baptist Church), a settlement which grew out of the post-Civil War sale of parcels of land to groups of freed people who had initially settled at Freedman's Village or the Georgetown section of Washington, D.C., where some of the thousands of fugitives who escaped to the Union lines during the war were housed. In the early stages of the community's development, Jones' home served as a school, a church, and a meeting house. When he died in 1886, his property remained in the family, under the control of his wife, Sarah, and their five children.

Nauck: Our Historic Community

Excerpts from *Community Voices, The Nauck Community Heritage Project, 2008*
- compiled by Dr. Alfred O. Taylor, Jr.

Nauck/Green Valley

It has been stated that it is doubtful that any of the early settlers of Northern Virginia made a more significant and large-scale contribution to the development of Arlington (and have received less credit and recognition for it) than the Fraser's of the Green Valley Estate. Anthony Fraser built Green Valley Manor in 1821 on what is now the Army-Navy Country Club. His great-grandfather was Daniel Fraser of Scotland, a nephew of Simon Fraser, the last man beheaded in the Tower of London in 1747. Daniel arrived in Virginia as a ship's stowaway. Daniel's son, William, is recorded as settling in Arlington in the mid-1700s as a tenant of the Alexander family of Abingdon, the plantation along the Potomac River whose ruins are located between the parking garages of the National Airport. William's son, William, Jr. (the father of Anthony), acquired from the Alexander family several hundred acres of land straddling lower Long Branch, a tributary of Four Mile Run. The lands were known as Green Valley, perhaps named for James Green, who lived on the land near the present location of the clubhouse at the Army Navy Country Club.

Green Valley Manor was cited in the floor of a valley about a hundred yards from Long Branch. The estate included what are now the Oakridge Elementary School, the Gunston Middle School, Shirley Park, and Arna Valley, as well as land from Pentagon City and the River Houses almost to the banks of Four Mile Run. In selecting the particular site for his home, Fraser must have been influenced by the existence of a productive spring, where he also built a spring house. It is recorded that long before the establishment of Green Valley Estates, George Washington stopped frequently at the spring for drinking water when inspecting his lands along Four Mile Run. Washington also stopped at the spring with his troops when moving through the area on his way to Yorktown in September 1781. From the high ridge above Fraser's manor and about a mile to the east, the Frasers could easily have seen Abingdon on the banks of the Potomac River. To the north, about two miles away (unless the view was blocked by trees), they could have seen the Arlington House mansion of George Washington Parke Custis, started in 1802 and completed in 1817, only a few years earlier.

When the Frasers first arrived in Green Valley, the area was rustic, undeveloped, largely forested, and unsettled. The closest dwellings, about where Pentagon City is now located, were three structures known as Awbrey's, Griffen's, and Wheeler's places. Across Four Mile Run and close to the Mount Vernon Avenue Bridge entrance to Alexandria, there were two structures: Chubb's House and Chubb's Mill. Around 1840 the Frasers acquired new neighbors with the arrival of James Roach and his family. They would build their home on Hoe Hill, which they renamed Prospect Hill, at the northern end of Arlington Ridge.

Once established at Green Valley Manor, the Fraser family steadily grew. Anthony and his wife, Presha Lee, had five daughters: Cornelia, Mary, Frances, Miranda, and Presha. Also included among their family group were two farmers, John Casey and Edward Clements, and two African American men (probably slaves), Nathan Butler and Douglas Jones. Fraser became a leader in local affairs and, on June 26, 1849, he was elected Overseer of the Poor, as recorded in the Minute Book of Alexandria County.

The Fraser properties were extensively occupied and used by the Union Army throughout most of the Civil War. Barracks for troops were erected in numerous places, as was Fort Richardson, one of the numerous forts built to protect the Capital from possible attacks from the south or west, and Fort Albany, on the high ground to the east. The earthworks and ditches of Fort Richardson now remain beside green number nine at the Army Navy Country Club. Additionally, a hospital and convalescent camp were established on Rapid Run where it empties into Long Branch. The late Arlington historian Templeman wrote that the run was renamed Bloody Run because it ran red with blood from the numerous amputations performed there. During this period, Fraser, steadily growing blind, was saddened to hear the constant chop of axes as Union soldiers worked through the night to fell the hundreds of trees on his land to clear fields of fire for the forts' guns, to obtain lumber for the construction of barracks and hospitals, and for firewood. He survived the war but died soon after in 1881 and was buried on his property. The Fraser family grave site is at Hole 26 on the Army Navy Golf Course.

In 1924 Green Valley Manor was destroyed by fire, originating from causes that have never been conclusively established. Frances Lee Sickles, the granddaughter of Fraser, and her daughter were in Paris at the time. Some foundations and parts of the fireplace and walls remained until modern times, almost completely concealed in the heavy overgrowth. One of the few items of furniture retrieved from the fire is a desk known as the "Desk of Infamy." Legend has it that the desk was once owned by Jefferson Davis, who used it when he penned his fatal refusal to consider a carte blanche request from President Lincoln to write his terms for ending the war, at a time when the losses on both sides had become overwhelming.

Free African Americans, Levi and Sarah Ann Jones, were among the first African Americans to establish themselves in what is now known as Nauck. They were landowners prior to the Civil War, and they built their home in 1844. The local community began to grow as the Jones family began selling some of their property to other African American families. Indeed, members of the Jones family were original owners of the land where Dunbar Homes (now Shirlington Crest at Nauck) was constructed in 1944.

The Nauck community is named for John D. Nauck, Jr., a resident of Washington, D.C., who bought forty-six acres of land in south Arlington in 1874 and began subdividing it. Prior to that time, the area was known as Green Valley, named for the Green Valley Manor, which was situated on a forty-six-acre farm at 23rd and Arlington Ridge Road and overlooked the current site of the Army Navy Country Club. People in the Nauck community continued to refer to the area as Green Valley, well into the middle of the twentieth century.

While the Nauck community's origins predate the Civil War, and African American families like the Jones family formed a seed for the future, the community's growth, particularly in the twentieth century, was fed by migration. In particular, Nauck became a station on a migration that traces to the end of the Civil War and the establishment of Freedman's Village in Arlington following the Emancipation Proclamation in 1863.

From its earliest days and throughout most—and particularly the first half—of the twentieth century, Nauck and other African American communities were largely excluded from full participation in mainstream American political and social life and commerce. As a result, communities had to "do for themselves." They made their own institutions, and they did their best to provide services for themselves and their neighbors. They also made their own fun. Community churches facilitated many of these activities. When the subject of community churches arises, people in Nauck tend to speak of four churches in particular: Lomax A.M.E. Zion (1866), Mount Zion Baptist (1866), Macedonia Baptist (1908), and Our Lady Queen of Peace Catholic Church (1947).

Like so many other services and facilities, schools in the Nauck community began as a local community initiative. The first school in the Nauck community opened in 1875 at the old Lomax Chapel, on what is now Shirlington Road. It came to be known as the Kemper School by 1883. The school board built a one-room school in 1885, and in 1893, a new, two-story brick school was constructed at South Lincoln Street (Kemper Heights Homes site). It was later replaced by a larger building built for Arlington's African American population in 1945, which came to be known as Kemper Annex. It was renamed in 1952 to honor Dr. Charles R. Drew. With the end of segregation in 1971, the Drew Model School became a countywide magnet school. The school was rebuilt in 2000. It now has a three-pronged mission: a community school and a countywide magnet school offering Montessori and traditional approaches to education.

There has always been an entrepreneurial spirit in the Nauck/Green Valley community, a spirit born of necessity. Community businesses represent efforts by local entrepreneurs to carve a living out in difficult or problematic social and economic times, which were, more or less, a standard feature of African American life from the Civil War onward. Nauck businesses, like so many other faces of the community, evolved in the shadow of segregation, and business people in Nauck stepped up to supply services to their community that were often denied to them. Nauck businesses provided services to the local community that were otherwise inaccessible—places to sit down and eat, to play, to purchase groceries, or to get a haircut or permanent. Small businesses and services catering to the needs of local people are a longtime feature of Nauck/Green Valley. Funeral homes, beauty parlors, food and grocery retailers, convenience stores, auto repair, restaurants, and other businesses have operated mostly along the Shirlington Road corridor.

The Nauck/Green Valley community made their own fun, too. In the early part of the twentieth century, they played baseball and football on fields made themselves at Peyton's Field, a property owned by the Peyton family but open to the community. Peyton's Field had a dance hall, motorcycle races, and baseball and football games. Arlington County acquired the property in the 1940s and changed the name to the Jennie Dean (famous African-American educator) Playground and retained the sports fields. As a result of the efforts of local people, the Veterans Memorial YMCA (now Macedonia Baptist Church Family Life Center) was dedicated in 1949. The Y featured a twenty-five-meter swimming pool and other recreational facilities. A whole range of activities, including dances and serialized movies, also took place at the community room in Dunbar Mutual Homes.

The question that remains for the Nauck community is: Where do we go from here? Will the community be able to hang on to its unique identity as it weathers the changes that development, migration, and gentrification will bring? The answers to these questions will be determined by local people's ability to build a coherent story of who they are as an integral community going forward; how they weave together the separate threads of their various identities as churchgoers, business people, educators, and community activists into one, whole cloth. It is our hope that, as the community grows, new chapters will be added to the story, and future generations and new residents will come to consider the history of the Nauck community their own.

Our Community School History:
Drew Model Elementary School

In 1669 John Alexander purchased forty-six acres, which was eventually sold to Anthony Fraser during the 1800s. His daughter, who married J. E. Sickles, inherited the property. It is said that a member of the Fraser-Sickles family who did not believe in slavery freed his slaves and gave them land, as well as money, to construct houses on the land. That area became known as Green Valley.

The community grew with the subdivision of land by John P. Nauck, Jr. (an upholsterer who was Justice of the Peace from 1890-91) and the movement of people from Freedmen's Village, where "freed [N]egroes" were settled by the Freedmen's Bureau after the Civil War. Freedmen's Village was actually the third such settlement. When President Lincoln freed all slaves in 1862, large numbers of impoverished slaves were homeless. What was in effect a concentration camp was established to house them on what is now the site of the Folger Library on East Capitol. A smallpox epidemic forced the removal of the camp to another site on 12th Street. But even here, conditions were deplorable. In May 1863, the Quartermaster of the Washington Military District recommended resettlement in the "pure country air" of the Arlington Plantation, on land which is now the southernmost part of Arlington Cemetery.

The first building of Lomax Church, formerly called the Little Zion A.M.E. Zion Church, was one which had been taken down in Freedmen's Village and re-erected at the new site. It had only one room where the congregation worshipped on Sunday, held its prayer and business meetings at night, and was the site of a public school during the day. The school in Lomax Chapel, which was rented for twenty-five dollars a year, was opened in 1875 because "certain colored men residents of Arlington requested another colored school be opened in order to be accessible to those living in the southern part of the district." It was located in the 2500 block of Shirlington Road which, at that time, may have been called Seminary Road. By 1883 it was being referred to as Kemper School, after James L. Kemper, then Governor of Virginia, who was an advocate of African American education.

The school board agreed on March 26, 1883, to buy three-fourths of an acre from J. D. Nauck for $62.50, for the purpose of building a school in the area. On July 8, 1885, it called for bids for constructing a frame, one-story, 24-by-36-foot building, to be completed by August 25. Mr. Hall's bid was accepted on July 15, and it was noted that the lease on the building theretofore used had expired. Mr. Hall met the deadline with time to spare and, on August 19, 1885, the new building was inspected, approved, and accepted by the Board. A few years later, Kemper School moved to Peyton Hall at 22nd and Kenmore. Macedonia Baptist Church had relocated to Peyton Hall because it had outgrown its church building. The church was housed upstairs and Kemper School on the lower level.

The next year, the board decided to build a new, two-story, brick structure for Kemper at a cost of $1,500. Originally only the two, lower rooms were used, but in 1903, the upper story was finished off for classrooms.

Kemper School was constructed by Noble Thomas, the first African American contractor of County public schools. Mr. Murray A. Richardson, who was interviewed for an oral history project stated:

> When we were suffering for leadership back in the early teens, we had a man come in to Arlington County by the name of Noble N. Thomas. When Noble Thomas started out, he was a court stenographer in Washington, where he was born. He married into the Jones family, Joe and Hattie Jones. He married their daughter, their only child. He came here to live. He started a hog farm, right there where the school is now. When World War I broke out, he wanted to join in the service, but they turned him down because he was doing essential work by being a hog farmer, so he ran the hog farm until after the war, and then he went into the contract[or] business full-time. He built South Gate off Queen Street at Johnson Hill. He was the first African American to build a public building in the State of Virginia. He built the school here at Kemper School. He built Hoffman-Boston at Johnson's Hill, and he built John M. Langston School at Halls Hill. He imported most of his laborers and brick-layers from North Carolina because there were none here in the County. He organized the first association of African American residents back in 1920, the Arlington County Colored Citizens.

Teacher turnover at Kemper School was exceptionally low. From 1881 through 1905, as far as the record goes, there were only four, different teachers. The first one, Miss Ida Grey, was appointed on August 6, 1881. Isaiah Hutton was first appointed on September 14, 1883, and served until the end of the school year in 1901. Mr. Hutton lived in the district and walked to and from school each day. He was not alone, as many children at that time walked from Virginia across Key Bridge to Wormley School on Prospect Street [Avenue] in Georgetown. On June 17, 1901, Sumner G. Holmes was appointed. His salary was five dollars a month less than that of his colleagues, and the explanatory note is inserted that this was in view of his youth. He was the son of the long-term Commissioner of the Revenue, H. L. Holmes. While he taught at Kemper, he was putting himself through medical school. Upon his graduation, he served as a well-known physician in Arlington until his death in 1930. Mr. Holmes was succeeded by Miss Ella Boston in 1904, with his sister, Miss Marie Holmes, as her assistant. According to the adopted budget of 1905-06, Miss Boston was to receive forty-five dollars a month and her assistant, thirty-five dollars. It is interesting that, in the beginning, all salaries in the County were the same, whether for men or women, for white or [N]egro teachers. Gradually distinction began to appear.

Around 1913 Ms. Ella Boston, who was then principal of Kemper School, talked to the Superintendent of Arlington Schools, Mr. Hodges, asking that she be permitted to add an eighth grade class of students. Mr. Hodges agreed. The four students were: Mr. Henson Thompson, Mr. Samuel Brown, Ms. Mary Fountain, and Ms. Marguerite West. Teachers were Mrs. Martha Gray, Mrs. Florence Johnson, and Mrs. Lillian Smackum, who later became principal.

In 1944 the Kemper Annex was erected on the old Gray homestead. The school had six teachers: Ms. Smackum, Ms. Hogue, Ms. Haskell, Ms. Hicks, Ms. Sydnor, and Ms. (Woodson) Ross. It also had six classrooms and two playrooms, one for girls and one for boys. World War II prevented Drew from being built sooner than it was. When a larger addition was built in 1951, the entire facility was renamed in honor of Dr. Charles Drew.

Reproduction of un-authored paper, dated May 1, 1989

Our Community Churches History

Our Lady Queen of Peace Catholic Church

The history of Our Lady Queen of Peace (OLQP) is written in the dedication, loyalty, hard work, and prayers of countless people who gave life to a dream. It represents the culmination of the courageous efforts of a small group of African American Catholics who took Jesus at His word and laid the foundation for a worshiping community that would welcome all as sisters and brothers and as members of the great family of God.

Our Lady Queen of Peace is an appropriate name for a parish that was born in 1945 at the end of World War II. Although African Americans had fought equally with other Americans during the war, racial segregation prevailed, both in the wider society and in the Catholic Church. African American Catholics in Arlington went to Mass and attended school in Washington, D.C. or at St. Joseph's, an African American Catholic Church in Alexandria, Virginia, which was established in 1915.

In the early 1940s, a group of devout and determined African American Catholics began plans to build a Catholic church where they could worship in dignity. By 1945 they were able to obtain a meeting with a representative of the Richmond Diocese, then responsible for Arlington County, to discuss establishing a parish for African American Catholics. The meeting took place in the home of Edward and Alice Moorman. The group became the founders of Our Lady Queen of Peace. They were: Joseph Bowman, Clarence and Selena Brown, Alice Butler, Lawrence and Jessie Butler, Irma Carter, Hattie Ellis, Mary Fernanders, Edward Marshall, Grace McGwinn, Edward and Alice Moorman, Constance Spencer, Sophia Terry, and Thaddenia West. Today all of the founding members are deceased, except for Thaddenia West, who is a living tribute to the founding of Our Lady Queen of Peace.

Bishop Ireton granted the request of the African American Catholics to establish their own church in Arlington County. He asked the Holy Ghost Fathers to minister to the parish, and they appointed Fr. Joseph Hackett as the first pastor. On Pentecost, on May 20, 1945, forty people and Fr. Hackett celebrated the first Mass in the home of Lawrence and Jessie Butler, located on South Barton Street. Subsequent services were held at the residence of Fr. Hackett, a home rented for him by the Holy Ghost Fathers. A new location was sought when it became obvious that the priest's residence could no longer accommodate the increasing number of parishioners. Through the efforts of Mr. Maurice Coates, a parishioner and manager of Dunbar Homes, the site of the Paul Lawrence Dunbar Homes in the Green Valley (Nauck) neighborhood became a temporary location for church services. He provided a small auditorium where Fr. Hackett began offering Mass. Later a site was found for the new church on South 19th and Edgewood Streets. Mr. Solomon Thompson, an African American real estate agent, and Mr. Clarence Brown, negotiated and purchased the property (under the auspices of the Diocese of Richmond), and plans began to construct a new church building.

During the first year of Our Lady Queen of Peace parish, the Holy Name Society, the Sodality, and the Junior Sodality were established. Holy Name officers were: Clarence Brown, John Phoenix Sr., and Joseph Bowman. Sodality officers were: Alice Moorman, Ruth Phoenix, and Roberta Wilson. The first altar boys, organized and trained by Edward Hicks, were: Clifton West, George Marshall, Leonard Lewis, Thomas and Bernard Fernanders, and Reginald Carter. On February 3, 1946, Cleo Butler and Guy Wills were the first couple whose marriage was recorded in the sacramental register at Our Lady Queen of Peace. The parishioners held many activities, such as dinners, bake sales, lawn parties, rummage sales, and teas to raise money for the parish.

After overcoming several, bureaucratic obstacles, one year and four months after celebrating their first Mass, parishioners of Our Lady Queen of Peace were granted approval to construct their church. On September 20, 1946, Alice Moorman, representing the Sodality, and Clarence Brown, representing the Holy Name Society, along with Fr. Hackett, turned the first shovels of soil, marking the groundbreaking for the new church. Father Stephen, of St. Mary Church in Alexandria, preached the sermon. On Pentecost Sunday, June 15, 1947, Bishop Peter Ireton dedicated Our Lady Queen of Peace Church. The Knights of St. John, an African American honor society, attended the Bishop. Joseph Thomas, organist and founder of the first choir, played for the dedication.

Many rituals and observances of a Christian community occurred in the new parish. Nuns from St. Mary's Academy, Alexandria, taught Sunday school. In June 1947, a summer school was started for twenty-six children, six of whom received First Communion on July 13, 1947. The first Confirmation took place in April 1948, with thirty candidates receiving the sacrament from Bishop Ireton. Patricia Lumpkins was Queen of the first May Procession in 1948.

In April 1948, Fr. Hackett was called to a new ministry and was succeeded by Fr. Michael Kanda. By the time Fr. Kanda arrived, the membership of Our Lady Queen of Peace had grown to approximately seventy-five to one hundred families. He provided transportation to Sunday school and organized a basketball team for church and neighborhood youth. Fr. Kanda was also instrumental in the integration of the boys' basketball teams of the diocesan Catholic Youth Organizations. He opened his heart and home to all boys and girls, regardless of race or religion and, as a result, many people in the neighborhood converted to Catholicism.

OLQP did not have an elementary school. Children attended Catholic schools in Alexandria or Washington, D.C. As a result of the 1954 Supreme Court's *Brown v. Board of Education* decision, Cardinal Patrick O'Boyle desegregated parochial schools in the Archdiocese of Washington. Two OLQP parishioners, Marguerite Thomas and W. Cassell Butler, both active in the Arlington NAACP, negotiated the entry of African American children into Arlington parochial schools in the early 1950s. The Thomas children (Keith, James, and Cecilia Thomas) integrated St. Thomas Moore School, and the Butler's child (Johnella Butler) integrated St. Charles. In the late 1950s, other schools desegregated by black children from the parish included St. Mary's Academy (Jackie and Veronica Alfred) and Archbishop O'Connell High School (Shuford Hill Jr. and Ronald Ricks).

From 1952 to 1958, a number of Holy Ghost Fathers served the parishioners of Our Lady Queen of Peace. Fr. Kanda was succeeded in 1952 by Fr. Thomas Jones, who was pastor until his death in 1955. Fr. James White was assigned as pastor for two years and, in 1958, was succeeded by Fr. Francis Smith. Later that year, Fr. David Ray was assigned and became the sixth pastor of Our Lady Queen of Peace. (Source: Excerpted from Internet Article) The community at Our Lady Queen of Peace continues to be a diverse one with a sense of welcome for all, which stems from its origin in 1945 as a black Catholic community.

Mount Zion Baptist Church

After the close of the Civil War, a number of Christians banded together to establish a Baptist church in Freedman's Village. This site is now the National Arlington Cemetery. They called this church the Old Bell Church. Members worshipped under the leadership of the first pastor, Reverend Robert S. Laws. When the federal government moved the congregation from this location, they settled in nearby Alexandria County, which is now Arlington County, Virginia. In September 1866, another space was purchased on Mt. Vernon Avenue, which was later named Arlington Ridge Road.

Here a new church was erected and named Mount Zion Baptist Church. This was a two-story, red brick building with a white marble front. Reverend Joseph Matthews served as pastor for fifteen years.

Reverend James E. Green was elected pastor in 1914, after many years of service. He joined Mount Zion in 1903. He served as superintendent of the Sunday school for three years and on the Deacon Board for nine years. He was a dynamic leader of the church and community. Under Reverend Green's pastorate, a new church was erected in 1930 at the Arlington Ridge Road site at a cost of $26,000.

Since 1866, Arlington's oldest black congregation has survived four relocations.

In 1942 the federal government condemned the property to make way for a network of roads. The Odd Fellows Hall at Columbia Pike and South Ode Street was selected as a temporary place of worship. Later property was purchased at 19th and Lowell Streets. Groundbreaking services were held on Easter Sunday, April 9, 1944. The first services were held in the new building on the first Sunday in July 1945.

In January 1952, Dr. Oswald G. Smith was elected pastor of the Mount Zion Baptist Church. Before coming to Mount Zion, he was assistant pastor at Metropolitan Baptist Church in Washington, D.C. Early in his ministry, he emphasized the role of community service in fulfilling the Mount Zion Church mission. In 1956 he established a Deacon's Fund to assist both members and non-members in meeting emergency costs for goods, medicine, shelter, utilities, and other necessities.

In March 1992, Dr. Leonard N. Smith was installed as the ninth senior minister. Under the leadership of Dr. Smith, the membership and stewardship has nearly doubled. More than 2,500 have united with Mount Zion, and the church budget has increased to over one million dollars. Mount Zion has purchased twenty-two acres of land in Woodbridge, Virginia, in order to further their mission to go and make disciples of all nations as we are commanded. While working together to realize the vision, Mount Zion continues to expand its outreach with food assistance and tutorial and financial support to community service agencies.

Lomax AME Zion Church

Lomas AME Zion Church was organized on June 12, 1866, in Freedom's Village located in Arlington Heights, which is now Arlington National Cemetery. During the Civil War, African Americans migrated to Washington from Maryland and Virginia in such great numbers that the U.S. Government made provisions for housing and security. General Robert E. Lee forfeited the land to the Federal Government, and by order of the Secretary of War, Edwin M. Stanton, set aside this land as home for "freed men." Many of our forefathers became self-sufficient by securing jobs as barbers, teamsters, servants, and farmers.

A handful of stalwart Christians organized Wesley Zion Church under the leadership of Reverend Richard Thompkins. The following persons were charter members of the church organization: Peter H. Jackson and William Marshall; local preachers Elious Plummer, Henry Swanigan, Isaac Wood, and Daniel Hogan; and trustees David Boyd, Class Leader, William Springsteen, Secretary and John Wells, Cornelius Young, Thomas Simms, Nicholas Snow, Henry Jackson, Mary Young, Eliza Hogan, Eliza Boyd, Rebecca Plummer, Mrs. Smith, Jane Oskins, and Eliza Thomas.

For some time, the congregation worshiped in Freedmen's Village, until they began to scatter to other locations. Many settled in this part of the County, which was known as Camp Distribution and later as Convalescent Camp. Prayer meetings and regular services were held in the homes of Mrs. Ann Jones and Mr. Henson Thompson, until Mrs. Jones made available to them a small frame building on her property, and the first church home was established, in which Miss V. Thompkins (daughter of Reverend Richard Thompkins) taught school. In 1874, the congregation led by Reverend L. Granderson Mitchell purchased land for a permanent home. The present site was selected by the late Wallace Boswell whose honored remains now rest in a hollowed spot as the front of the church. Mr. Boswell was affectionately called "neighbor" by the members of this community.

On August 8, 1874, the first payment of five dollars (provided by Reverend L. Granderson Mitchell and Mrs. Julia Swanigan) was paid on this property toward the purchase price of seventy five dollars. The last payment was made on February 29, 1876. At that time, the church was called Little Zion AME Zion Church.

In May 1876, Bishop T. H. Lomax was elected Bishop and assigned to this district, and it was then that the membership renamed the church Lomax AME Zion Church.

The first building erected on this site was taken down in Freedmen's Village and rebuilt here. It was a crude, one-room, framed building made of twelve-inch boards. For approximately one year, the congregation worshipped in this building on Sunday and held prayer and business meetings. Public school was held during the weekdays and during evening hours.

Reverend Granderson Mitchell was followed in succession by Reverends J. Watters; R. R. Johns; A. J. Hollard; J. Saunders; A. C. Washington; C. C. Perkins; T. G. Campbell; M. M. Bell; W. H. Wright; G. Bosley; T. Jenkins; B. H. Freeman; W. H. Smith; L. Clayton; W. L. Holland; A. Washington; A. Hannam; W. Alexander; J. Green; C. Madox; J. A. Jones; J. Lee; A. Day; N. H. Williams; J. A. Russell; J. Swann; R. Nelson; C. Wye; and S. S. Swann.

In 1887 the cornerstone was laid for the second chapel, under the leadership of Reverend J. S. Waters. Mr. Tibbit Allen served as the Chairman of the Board of Trustees. The building was completed in 1889 and was called Lomax Chapel of the AME Zion Church. The church continued to grow spiritually, financially, and in membership. Lomax Chapel was the center of all interests in the community.

During the pastorate of the Reverend F. R. Killingsworth, the congregation built another structure, this time a brick edifice. On October 29, 1922, the cornerstone, a gift from Dr. Laura Killingsworth, wife of the pastor, was laid. It was mainly through the efforts of the members of the Board of Trustees, men of sterling qualities, that this building became a reality.

The following trustees each gave five hundred dollars toward the building of this church: S. H. Thompson; L. L. Gray; T. H. West; and C. E. Offutt. The other trustees and members made large contributions, as attested by the fact that although the building cost $29,000 to erect, only $10,000 remained to be paid when the building was occupied. The trustees under the chairmanship of Mr. Thompson maneuvered to get the building in the Fairfax Building and Loan Association.

The history of the Lomax AME Zion Church is highlighted by the devotion of Christian men and women who were never satisfied with the status quo. Each succeeding generation has had a solid foundation upon which to stand and the inner fervor of undaunted spirits as a source of inspiration. The spot upon which Lomax stands today is hallowed by the lives of martyrs. It is made sacred by the contributions of those who searched for a city and whose builder and maker is God.

Macedonia Baptist Church

Prayer gatherings in the home of Bonder and Amanda Johnson in 1908 led to the formal establishment of the Macedonia Baptist Church in Arlington, Virginia, in 1911 by Reverend Brass Clark of Alexandria and Reverend Frank Graham of the Mount Zion Baptist Church. Reverend John Gilliam served as the church's first pastor. During the period from 1912 until 1923, the church was served by the following: Reverend Williams, Reverend Peter Mitchell, Reverend Bernard Botts, Reverend Pickney, Reverend Richardson, Reverend Carter Taylor, and Reverend Oliver Hawkins.

After outgrowing their original home, the congregation purchased its first building, the old Peyton Hall at Nauck Station under the pastorate of Reverend Bernard Botts. During the years 1923 to 1968, the pastorate was served by Reverend Sherman W. Phillips, who served faithfully for forty-five years.

Under his pastorate, the growth in membership resulted in the construction of a new edifice at the corner of 22nd Street and the "Track" (Kenmore Street), where the cornerstone was laid on September 18, 1927.

Reverend Clarence A. Robinson succeeded Reverend Sherman W. Phillips as the pastor on February 26, 1969. Under his leadership, the expansion program was initiated, and on October 10, 1971, the cornerstone was laid by the Grand Lodge of Virginia and Arlington Lodge #58. On February 26, 1995, a final pastoral worship service was held, and Reverend Robinson officially retired after twenty-six years of dedicated ministerial service to Macedonia Baptist Church and the Nauck Community.

On July 18, 1996, the membership of Macedonia Baptist Church rendered a 97 percent "affirmative vote" of those "present and voting" in the election of Dr. Leonard L. Hamlin, Sr., as the pastor-elect. In November 1996, Dr. Hamlin was installed and given full, pastoral authority. Under the profound pastoral leadership of Dr. Hamlin, Macedonia Baptist Church has been praising God for numerous blessings and witnessed the following:

❖ Continuous growth in church membership, approximately 1,300-plus members;
❖ Major renovations of the upper level of the church;
❖ Purchase of the following properties: 2112; 2114; 2218; 2219; and 2229 South Shirlington Road;
❖ Purchase of the former Veteran's Memorial YMCA building, later renamed the Macedonia Baptist Church Family Life Center;
❖ Purchase of twenty-four and fifteen-passenger buses;
❖ Establishment of the Bonder and Amanda Johnson Community Development Corporation;
❖ Establishment of forty-four ministries;
❖ Partnership with the Affordable Housing Corporation for the development of thirty-six affordable housing units, opened under the name, the Macedonian, in May 2011. The Macedonian provided thirty-six new affordable apartments in the Nauck community of Arlington, Virginia. Five units were dedicated to Arlington County's Supportive Housing Program for persons with disabilities. The building includes more than two thousand square feet of commercial office space for the Bonder and Amanda Johnson Community Development Corporation (BAJCDC) and planned office space for a business incubator. The property is being provided by Macedonia Baptist Church through a sixty-five-year ground lease. Apartment rents are set at 50 percent and 60 percent of the Area Median Income (AMI);
❖ Under his pastorate there have been fourteen ministers licensed, five ministers ordained, sixteen deacons ordained, and twenty-three deaconesses consecrated; and
❖ Under his pastorate, three associate ministers have become pastors of area congregations.

The Macedonia Baptist Church, under its present, pastoral leadership, continues to be a beacon in the historical Nauck neighborhood, as it holds true to its mission of: "Transforming Lives through the Discipleship of Jesus Christ," while keeping focus of its vision: "Becoming Active Disciples through Commitment, Witness, Love, and Relationship." (Source: Excerpted from Internet)

Our Nauck/Green Valley Bridge Builders

The biographical and/or stories included in this publication are mostly taken from the Internet or from self-reported stories and is not intended to be an accurate portrayal of that person. The editor's intention in this publication is to identify persons, both living and dead who, in his opinion, have led to the Nauck/Green Valley neighborhood becoming one that is attempting to grow in its diversity, while always remembering the "Bridge Builders," who toiled despite some of the obstacles blocking their movement to where it is today as one of Arlington's most desirable neighborhoods.

Dr. Alfred O. Taylor, Jr. (2013)

Business Owners

Tyra La'Nise Baker Thompson
Leonard (Doc) Muse (Green Valley Pharmacy)
Robert and Charles Bryant
Leon Hawkins
Hattie Berger Oliver
Cleveland C. James, Sr.
Sterling H. Harris
Leonard L. Gray
Henry B. Dean
Thomas H. West
George W. Bullock, Sr.
Jacob Robinson
Floyd A. Hawkins
James Turner Gaskill, Sr.
Mamie Bell Mackley Brown
Richard Walker
Kenneth A. (Kenny) Cooper
Elizabeth W. Green
Dale Harris
George Elliott
Robert and Rupert Baker
Ralph D. Collins, Sr.
George Moore
Marie Mosby
Verna Lee (Taylor) Dean
Lena Lachelle "Shelly" Baker-Scott

Tyra La'Nise Baker-Thompson

Tyra Baker was born on November 6, 1969, to Robert B. Baker, Jr. and Hazel Ernestine Baker. She has one sister and two brothers. She was educated in Arlington, Virginia. Ms. Baker graduated from Yorktown High School. Ms. Baker attended Howard University and graduated from The University of the District of Columbia with a degree in mortuary science. While attending Yorktown, she was very involved in DECA and was vice president of the club. She became a model at Barbizon School and a fashion consultant for a new teenage store chain called County Seat. She would model clothes and represent them on panels; for this accomplishment she received an award from the school board in 1986.

Ms. Baker has worked in some capacity at Chinn Funeral Service as she was able to in her teen years. She has been working there, helping to run the day-to-day operations, for nineteen years. Her work includes coordinating funerals, facilitating paperwork, consoling the bereaved, and assisting families in need. It is her calling to be there for families in their time of need. She is very compassionate and helps her families through their time of bereavement. People admit seeing her smiling face is soothing to them.

In addition to her duties with Chinn Funeral Service, Ms. Baker is very involved in the community as a civic activist and a representative for her neighborhood school. She accepted the Abbey Award for Excellence Service to the community for Chinn Funeral Service in 2004. Along with The Martin Luther King Center, she has fed people for Thanksgiving and given kids clothing and toys for Christmas. She has served on several boards that represent the Nauck neighborhood and their needs. She has also served the community on NAACP committees. She gives of herself wholeheartedly in everything she does. She has helped women to get back on their feet with housing and job placement and will be working with the Bonder and Amanda Johnson CDC and Nauck United to help people realize their dreams of employment and housing.

She has been an election official for twenty-two years, and for the last fifteen years, she has been the Chief of Arlington Precinct 30. She is now an assistant registrar for Arlington County government.

Ms. Baker has been an intricate part of the revitalization process in the Nauck Neighborhood. She has been the chairperson since its inception in 2001. She was appointed by the county board to head up this process. It has been very successful.

She is married, living in the Nauck Green Valley, and raising her children. In 2001 she married the love of her life, Carleton "Tony" Thompson, a man from the neighborhood. Together they have twins, (born on September 11, 2001), Trey and Trent Thompson, and a daughter, Taylor, who was born during the blizzard of 2003. She has a son, Markies Eric Hart, Jr., and a stepson, Carleton A. Thompson, Jr. (Source: Tyra Baker-Thompson Submission)

Leonard (Doc) Muse (Pharmacist)

The only lunch counter where African Americans could eat was in the Green Valley Pharmacy, started by Leonard Muse, the first African American pharmacist in Virginia. Mr. Muse and his pharmacy are still open seven days a week.

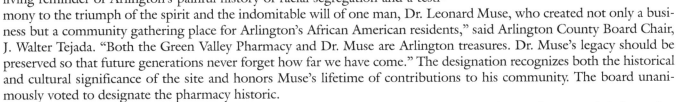

The Arlington County Board designated the Green Valley Pharmacy, in the Nauck neighborhood, as the 33rd Arlington Historic District. Green Valley Pharmacy is the County's longest, continuously operating, African American-owned pharmacy. Its owner, Dr. Leonard Muse, opened the pharmacy in 1952 to serve African Americans who, during that time of racial segregation, were not served by the County's white-owned pharmacies.

"Green Valley Pharmacy is both a living reminder of Arlington's painful history of racial segregation and a testimony to the triumph of the spirit and the indomitable will of one man, Dr. Leonard Muse, who created not only a business but a community gathering place for Arlington's African American residents," said Arlington County Board Chair, J. Walter Tejada. "Both the Green Valley Pharmacy and Dr. Muse are Arlington treasures. Dr. Muse's legacy should be preserved so that future generations never forget how far we have come." The designation recognizes both the historical and cultural significance of the site and honors Muse's lifetime of contributions to his community. The board unanimously voted to designate the pharmacy historic.

Green Valley Pharmacy is a simply designed, one-story building with minimal architectural accents. It is located at 2415 Shirlington Road at 24th Road South. Built in 1942 as a grocery store by the Hyman family, the building is within central Nauck, a community dating back to the mid-nineteenth century that is rich in African American history.

Dr. Muse opened the pharmacy at a time when Arlington was racially segregated. It became a successful business that served the greater Nauck area, along with other service-oriented African American-owned businesses, such as Naomi's T.V., Chinn's Funeral Home, and the Friendly Cab Company. These businesses provided much-needed services to the local African American community and continue to thrive today.

"It is an honor to leave my legacy, which has contributed to the cultural development of Arlington's African American community," said Dr. Leonard Muse. "I am proud to have been such a positive force in the growth of diversity in Arlington."

In the early 1950s, Muse and his initial business partner and former Howard University classmate, Waverly Jones, realized that there was a critical need for a pharmacy in Arlington, as no existing pharmacy in the County would serve African Americans. Muse and Jones opened the pharmacy in September 1952. Muse became the sole proprietor in 1955.

Muse's business remains one of the largest stores in Nauck, serving customers of all races and ages. He still offers affordable prices, door-to-door prescription delivery service, and daily meals at the dine-in food counter. The friendly atmosphere and camaraderie make the Green Valley Pharmacy both a popular and cherished symbol of Nauck's history and a favorite community gathering spot.

The Green Valley Pharmacy is the first historically African American commercial building to be honored as an Arlington Historic District. It is also the second local historic district to be created within the past year; Calloway Cemetery became a designated historic site in March 2012. Both sites provide important links to the cultural and historical contributions of Arlington's African American heritage. (Source: Excerpted from Internet article)

Robert and Charles Bryant

Robert and Charles Bryant were born in Palmetto, Georgia, to the late James and Oda Bell Bryant. The family moved north in 1939, and they grew up in Arlington, Virginia. They all attended the Lomax AME Zion Church. They received their education in both the Arlington County and Washington, D.C. Public School Systems. They received their high school diplomas from Armstrong High School and continued their education at Howard University, both graduating with degrees in architecture. Charles was a football player and was a top pole-vaulter.

After working as an architect for private firms and for the Veterans Administration and the General Services Administration, he opened his practice as Charles Irving Bryant Architects in 1965. In the late 1960s, he belonged to a frontier club who built affordable housing in Washington, D.C., off 14th Street. In 1969 the firm was renamed Bryant and Bryant Architects after Robert joined the firm. In 1976 the then fifty-person firm was cited in *Black Enterprise Magazine* as being the largest African American-owned firm in the nation and one of the top-ranked, African American-owned businesses in the nation, based on annual revenues.

Bob (Robert) and Charles were inducted into the College of Fellows of the American Institute of Architects, the highest recognition that an architect can receive from his peers.

The firm engaged in large-scale, master planning work, served as executive architects and planners on the Fort Lincoln, a new townhouse project in Washington, D.C., and engaged in similar work in Ghana and South America. They have executed more than seven hundred projects in the Washington Metropolitan Area, as well as throughout the United States and overseas. This includes the $100 million University of the District of Columbia; the 1,800-student replacement campus of the old Dunbar High School (The Fine Arts Commission singled it out for its innovative motif.); the Metropolitan Baptist Church of Washington, D.C.; the Howard Plaza Housing; the Richmond Exhibition Center; the Lomax parsonage; the Lomax Education Center; and the original plans for the current parsonage and the Macedonia Baptist Church in Arlington, Virginia.

They designed commercial office buildings, shopping centers, rapid transit stations, waste treatment centers, and recreation centers. Robert was also recognized in *Who's Who in America, Who's Who among Black Americans*, and *Who's Who in the East*. Robert was an architect engineer. He died in 1995. Charles was an architect draftsman and designer. He died in 2005. (This report was given by their sister, Mrs. Frances Sellers.)

Hattie Berger Oliver

African Americans were banned from white-owned restaurants, but they could eat at Hattie Oliver's fish dinner at the Shady Dale Restaurant. Mrs. Oliver did all the shopping, dish washing, and cooking herself.
Photos courtesy of Dr. Nancy Perry and John Robinson Collection

Hattie Melba was born in Hurt, Virginia, on May 29, 1921. She was the sixth of ten children born to the late Will and Hattie Doyle Berger. Melba was baptized at an early age at the New Mehundley Baptist Church.

Hattie raised two daughters and a son in Green Valley. This was during Segregation, so her children went to the local African American schools, starting at Kemper. When Kemper School was torn down to make way for some apartment buildings, the children moved to Drew School and then to Hoffman-Boston High School. Hattie grew up and went to school in Lynchburg, Virginia. When she first moved in Arlington, she rented a room from the sister-in-law of the man who owned the Shady Dale, a restaurant on Shirlington Road (the site of the current Martin Luther King Center), and supported herself by doing domestic work. In those days, it was not difficult for a young woman to find casual employment doing domestic work.

In 1942 the owner of the Shady Dale decided to get out of the restaurant business, so he put the Shady Dale up for rent. Hattie's first daughter was nine months old, and

her husband was working two custodian jobs, one at Buckingham and the other at the Washington Navy Yard. He and his business partner decided to take over operation of the Shady Dale. However, working two jobs and running the restaurant eventually became too much for her husband, so Hattie took his place, joining the business partner in running the restaurant. At first she was doing the dish washing and the partner was doing the cooking, but soon they decided that Hattie was the better cook, so she took over all the cooking responsibilities. Eventually Hattie assumed all the responsibilities of running Shady Dale from the business partner. She did all the shopping, cooked all the food, and washed all the dishes. Hattie remembered walking to the store to get groceries for the restaurant. It was a small enough operation that she could keep the pantry stocked if she shopped every other day. The only deliveries were beer from the beer distributor. Hattie's menu generally included potato salad, greens, and fish. She also sold a lot of sandwiches.

Her biggest days were Fridays, Saturdays, and Sunday afternoons after church. On Sundays she didn't open the restaurant until 1:00 P.M., but she still sold a lot of Sunday dinners. Her Friday fish dinners were so popular that she had to go to the waterfront early on Friday mornings to buy fish by the bushel. Her cooking was well-known by some of the employees at the Pentagon. They called her on Friday mornings to place their orders for the fish dinner. Hattie and her sister worked hard to get the meals ready. There were no carryout Styrofoam trays to carry the food, so Hattie piled it up on paper plates and wrapped them up in waxed paper. The offices would send someone down to the Shady Dale at lunchtime to pick up their dinners.

Hattie mentioned that her 'competition' was mostly families who sold food from their homes. Their customers would come to the front door, sit at the dining room table, and eat what the lady of the house prepared for them. Most of these little restaurants were only open a few days a week. There were a lot of little family restaurants, especially on Johnson's Hill. Hattie remembered that the ladies who ran the little restaurants were good cooks.

Hattie's customers were mostly African Americans. In addition to the Pentagon employees who bought her fish dinner every Friday, a lot of families came to get carryout on Friday evenings. On Saturdays and on Sunday afternoons, when people had a little more time to linger, they came to eat at the Shady Dale. The restaurant was a popular destination after baseball games, whether the Green Valley Black Sox won or lost. The only times Hattie saw white folks at the Shady Dale were on snow days. She had an agreement with the county employees working at the Arlington County property yard. On snow days, when there was no traffic moving, except the snowplows, Hattie opened the Shady Dale so the snowplow drivers, African American and white, had someplace to go to catch a meal.

Hattie had a second daughter while she was running the Shady Dale, and then a son. Running the restaurant and caring for three children was more than she could handle, so Hattie stopped running the restaurant. The new proprietors of the Shady Dale hired Hattie to cook for them, but they were not as successful as Hattie had been, and they were finally forced to close down the Shady Dale. For a while, Hattie cooked for the lunch counter at one of the little white-owned grocery stores in Green Valley. Finally she got a job cooking at the Three Chefs restaurant on Columbia Pike. Hattie spent much of her adult life cooking for others. She was a good cook. Mrs. Oliver passed in 2013. (Excerpts from an interview by Nancy Perry on July 5, 2010)

Cleveland C. James, Sr. (Delicatessen Owner)

On Tuesday, March 1, 2005, Cleveland C. James Sr., surrounded by his loving family, in Daytona Beach, Florida, quietly and peacefully slipped away from this earthly home to his heavenly home to be reunited with his angel, Mary. He was born March 20, 1926, to the late Eugene and Mamie James, and was preceded in death by his loving wife, Mary Louise James.

He was retired as a supervisor from the Defense Printing Department of the Pentagon and also established the James Delicatessen in Arlington, Virginia. Mr. James was also a Lecturer at the Washington Technical Institute (now UDC), where he taught bindery operations part-time in the Printing and Publishing Department. He was a life-long, dedicated member of St. Johns Baptist Church in Arlington, where he served in many capacities, including Trustee Board and Chairman of the Deacon Board. He was instrumental in leading the church, both spiritually and financially, and always believed in maintaining strong lines of communication.

Deacon James also had strong community involvement and, amongst his numerous affiliations, he was a founding member of the Arlington Community Action Program and the Nauck Civic Association; he served on the board of the local YMCA; and he held membership in Kiwanis and the Arlington Lodge #58 of the Free and Accepted Masons. He has received several, well-deserved recognitions and honors. (Source: Excerpted from obituary program from the Internet.)

Leon Hawkins (Window Cleaning & Maintenance Company)

Leon Hawkins was born on May 16, 1931, in Washington, D.C. He was the seventh child of ten children born to Floyd and Beatrice B. Hawkins in the District of Columbia. His education began in Arlington, Virginia, and then to Francis Junior High and Phelps Vocational High Schools in the District of Columbia.

Afterwards Leon enlisted in the U.S. Army in 1950 and was assigned to the 11th Airborne Division. He made ninety-four parachute jumps while stationed at Fort Campbell, Kentucky, and in Stuttgart, Germany. That is where he developed an affinity for the air and heights, thus desiring to clean windows on tall buildings. After three years in the service, he went to work for U.S. Windows Cleaners, where he asked for—and was not granted—a higher position, so he quit and started his own business. He attended some business seminars and founded Hawkins Window Cleaning and Maintenance Company and, for his own security, had it incorporated. Many of his coworkers from U.S. Window Cleaners came to work for him, along with three of his brothers. His parents manned the telephones and did the banking for him, while he obtained contracts and gave estimates on big jobs. His greatest desire and objective was to give work or find jobs for the underprivileged and jobless. In the summer, his sons worked for him and wanted him to hire all their friends who needed jobs, and he did. Many of his nieces and nephews were hired between jobs, and he hired many men from the Martin Luther King, Jr. Center. Some of his major contracts were with Gallaudet and American Universities, the N.S.A., and the C.I.A. (when newly constructed), the Watergate (D.C. and Virginia), and Cafritz Developments. After more than thirty years of service, he sold his business to a business associate, Edna Williams.

He has held membership in BSCAI (Building Service Contractors Association International), the Arlington Chamber of Commerce, the Jack & Jill Society of America, and the 19th Street Block Club of Nauck. Leon's hobby is working with plants and flowers (a green thumb inherited from his mother). He used to play football and golf and now enjoyed watching them on T.V. He loved playing chess and card games with his sons, family, and friends.

Leon was married to the former Naomi Yvonne Gillis and has two sons, Derrick and Sean of Arlington and two granddaughters and one grandson. (Source: Family document)

Sterling H. Harris (Builder)

Mr. Sterling H. Harris was born in Manassas, Virginia. He received his education in the Manassas Schools. He later came to Arlington where he began his contracting business. Many of the beautiful structures in Arlington and the surrounding areas were built by him. One of the most beautiful edifices that he constructed is the Mt. Zion Baptist Church. Mr. Sterling Harris was always a very active member in the St. John Baptist Church, where he served very faithfully; he was on the trustee board and was also a member of the choir for many years.

Leonard L. Gray (Builder)

Mr. Leonard L. Gray was a son and member of a pioneer family of Nauck. He was an outstanding citizen who contributed much to the community up-building. He greatly loved and valued the friendship of his fellowmen. His vast experience while working as a carpenter's helper at the Government Experimental Farm enabled him in later years to branch out in the field of contracting and building. He was a Trustee of the Lomax AME Zion Church, where he supervised the building of the present structure. Many homes in Nauck were built by him. He was a member of the Odd Fellows of Arlington. (Source: Internet Search)

Henry B. Dean (Paper Hanger)

Henry Dean was born on June 8, 1890, in Washington, D.C., and he resided for many years in the southeast section of the city. His vocations were in the manual field. He engaged in construction work, cement finishing, tile installation, paper hanging, painting, etc. He was also employed in the construction of the 14th Street Bridge.

After moving to Arlington, Virginia, he moved his membership from the Pilgrim Baptist Church in Washington, D.C. to the Macedonia Baptist Church under the pastorate of the late Reverend Sherman W. Phillips. There he was a faithful, dedicated member of the Board of Deacons, President of the senior choir, and President of the male chorus for many years. His manual skills were utilized in the Nauck community for many years. (Source: Obituary)

Thomas H. West (Builder)

Thomas Henry West (born in 1868) married Anne Rowe (born in 1869) and settled in what is now the Nauck community in the late 1800s. Thomas and Anne raised their eight children in Nauck. They owned enough property to give each of their children land on which to build. Some of the property was acquired through his wife, a descendent of William Rowe, and the balance he purchased. By occupation Mr. West was a general contractor and is credited with building several homes and churches in Nauck, Mclean, and Lyons Village. His colonial-style homes are characterized by large, columned front porches with central hallways that run through the front of the house to the back; a design that facilitates the flow of air. He also built bungalows characterized by a hip-type roof. Thomas West was also a trunk farmer who supplied produce to local grocery stores, including A&P. He often bought back delicacies from these stores, such as lobster, which was given to him either as partial payment for his products or for free.

He built homes in close proximity to his home on what is now Shirlington Road for five of his children, creating a family compound that included, at one time, eighteen grandchildren out of the thirty-two he eventually had. The proximity of the families created strong, family ties that still exist today. Everything was shared: food, clothing, time, work, and fun. Mr. West built a clay tennis court (at what is now South 23rd Street and Glebe Road) for his children; games, such as croquet, were played together, adults and children alike. Each of the children and later, his grandchildren, were expected to complete daily chores before school and on weekends. On Sundays everyone would gather after church for iced tea and cake, and they would sing Christian songs and play games on his expansive lawn. By most standards, his home was well-maintained. A&T filmed one of its commercials at his family home. The singer, Roberta Flack, also from Nauck, was featured in the commercial. As a side note, there was a streetcar that rode up and down Kenmore Street from Rosslyn. It turned around at South 24th Street. Mr. West's grandchildren would help the driver turn the cars around, and as a show of appreciation and for fun, they could ride the streetcar for free up to Glebe Road.

His family was very important to him, so he often took them with him on his jobs; not just to help, but to also make sure they learned a skill. He was progressive for his time. He taught his daughters, as well as his sons and grandsons, the intricacies of carpentry and business, such as selecting good wood, delivering a finished product, customer relations, pricing work, and planning ahead. The family, both girls and boys, assisted in the preparation of salt herring in barrels for winter meals; canning vegetables and fruits; repairing and maintaining the family homes; and preparing the soil for the family vegetable and flower gardens. In addition to teaching them how to cook and how to play the piano and the harp, his wife taught them etiquette, manners, and chivalry, arts that are lost in today's society. Anne Rowe West was an educator and placed emphasis on seeing that her children and grandchildren received a decent education. Because there were no African American high schools in Arlington, her children and grandchildren attended classes daily in Washington, D.C. high schools. The family network shared in transportation arrangements to the schools, including an almost-daily cab for five grandchildren to Washington, D.C. Their social life outside the family centered on the church and the immediate community of Nauck. Mr. West served as a type of welcome wagon in the community. When new families relocated to Nauck, they would be greeted with a supply of food and items he thought they would need that he could provide. Mr. West was one of the builders and major financial supporters of Lomax AME Zion Church and helped to build the structure that is standing today. His family carried on his tradition of community engagement by leading or actively supporting such activities as:

1. Organizing a social club in Nauck for girls
2. Organizing weekly entertainment for the sick and shut-in at local hospitals through the American Red Cross
3. Organizing integrated teen social events to ease the transition for the integration of the schools
4. Supporting the establishment of a church school
5. Serving as a missionary in foreign countries
   (Source: Yolanda Black, granddaughter)

George W. Bullock, Sr. (Hauling)

Mr. George W. Bullock, Sr. was born in Vance County, North Carolina, in 1885 and came to Arlington County in 1926. He has been in the hauling business in Arlington since 1932 and had employed several persons during that time. Mr. Bullock was one of the first African Americans to enter the hauling business in Arlington County.

Jacob Robinson (Upholsterer)

In 1938 Jacob Robinson began a furniture repair and re-upholstery business in a shed in his backyard. He serviced countless customers with projects from furniture repair, refinishing antiques, and re-staining to designing and upholstery from that shed for many years. Then he and his son, E.C. Robinson Sr., opened up a shop in North Arlington on Lee Highway named Robinson & Son's Upholstery. The business remained at that location for many years.

After Jacob retired, his son, E.C. Robinson Sr., took over the family business and renamed it E.C. Robinson Upholstery. Now located in Del Ray, Alexandria, the business is under the leadership of his son, E.C. Robinson, Jr. Now in its third generation of a family-owned operation, the Robinson family served clients in the Virginia and D.C. Metropolitan Area for more than seventy years with fine craftsmanship and value.

Floyd A. Hawkins (Bee Keeper)

Mr. Floyd A. Hawkins, Sr. was born in 1895, and first moved with his family to Arlington on a two-acre plot of land in 1925. While working as a letter carrier, and later a motor vehicle office supervisor at the Washington, D.C. City Post Office, Hawkins raised and sold meat from pigs, chickens, and turkeys from his Arlington farm. In 1930 he acquired his first bee hives. Over the next fifty-eight years, he was affiliated with numerous beekeeper's associations, won awards and ribbons, and conducted numerous classes in beekeeping through the Arlington 4-H.

At the age of eighty-one, Floyd Hawkins helped start the first Arlington County Fair in 1977, and served as the Fair's treasurer for ten years. In 1985 he was honored as a civic activist in Arlington County for over thirty thousand hours of volunteer service. He was also a member of St. John's Baptist Church and the Arlington Chapter of the Full Gospel Businessmen's Fellowship; a charter member of the Y Men's Club International and the Nauck Citizen's Association; and a past vice president of the Northern Virginia Beekeepers Association and the NAACP.

This quote is from his oral history, which patrons can read or hear in the Virginia Room:

"I started raising bees in 1930. I got two beehives, and they had got mean and wild at that time, you know, because they hadn't been attended to. So I got started off with two, mean beehives... [T]he queen bee, she's fertile for life. If she's mated by a gentle drone, every egg that she lays will be gentle bees, you see. If she's mated with a wild drone, the bees will be mean as long as she lives. She'll always lay those same eggs because she's fertile for life. So that's the way that they had gotten wild and mean, and I got them, and I got rid of the mean queen and ordered a gentle queen, and the bees became gentle.

"A colony of bees, that's one family. She's the mother of all. She can be the mother of a quarter of a million bees in her lifetime. That covers a span of about two years before she stops."
(Source: Family Supplied Document by Daughter-in-Law)

James Turner Gaskill, Sr. (Home Builder, Early Affordable Housing Builder)

James Turner Gaskill, Sr. was the sixth child born to the union of the late John Clement Gaskill, Sr. and the late Armania Drucilla Gaskill on May 22, 1933, in Yonkers, New York. He had six siblings: Edith, Drucilla, John Jr., Alease, Robert, and Warren. His early years of education were in the Detroit, Michigan, Washington, D.C., and Arlington, Virginia, Public School Systems. He graduated from Hoffman-Boston High School in Arlington, Virginia, in 1952. While at Hoffman-Boston, he was a member of the basketball team and was known as "Crazy Legs." James was a member of Omega Psi Phi Fraternity, Inc. at Virginia State University, where he majored in industrial management. He was a fervent member of the Omega Choraleers of Nu Psi Chapter of the Omega Psi Phi Fraternity, Inc. While at Virginia State, he was the "go-to" person because of his maturity, industriousness, creativity, and ability to problem-solve. He was married to Mrs. Jane Minor-Gaskill. This union produced one son, James T. Gaskill, Jr.. He also had one grandchild, James T. Gaskill, III.

James began working very early in life. He delivered newspapers for the Evening and Sunday Star (a Washington, D.C. newspaper) from 1939 to 1945. He then worked as a clerk/handyman at the Green Valley Market from 1942 to 1949. As a student at Virginia State University from 1952 to 1956, he worked at Phil's Grill and cleaned campus offices. On weekends, back in Arlington, James worked as a dishwasher, waiter, and chef at Dun-Movin, a small, African American-owned restaurant on Glebe Road in South Arlington. He was family referred to the owners, William and Katherine Hawkins, as "Lil Dun." Many distinguished African Americans from the Greater Washington, D.C. area frequented Dun-Movin. In 1956 James began his thirty-two-year career with the U.S. Postal Service, where he was a mail carrier with a general delivery route in the area of South Arlington. Concurrent with his postal career, James began his entrepreneurial effort, which was building, selling, and renting houses in South Arlington. He built or remodeled approximately forty homes.

Capitalizing on his work experience at Dun-Movin, his own interest in good food, and his insight regarding another business opportunity, he developed a food catering service. He had an excellent reputation for outstanding, home-style cooking, including mouth-watering desserts and his thirst quenching iced tea.

James was a member of the Lomax A.M.E. Zion Church, where he was a member of the Lay Council, Life Members, Sunday school faculty, men's chorale, Finance Committee and Chairperson of the Trustee Board. In retirement James enjoyed giving back. One service that he engaged in for many years was the full-course meals at Lomax Church. He and his efficient team offered meals to everyone, whether they were members or just looking for a good meal. James enjoyed spending time in the Charlotte, North Carolina, and Fort Lauderdale, Florida, areas. While in Fort Lauderdale, he attended Shaw Temple A.M.E. Zion Church, where he taught Bible study and assisted in training stewards, class leaders, and trustees. At the time of his death on June 9, 2013, he was a vital part of the Shaw Temple Building Fund Project. (Source: Document supplied by son, James Turner Gaskill, Jr.)

Mamie Bell Mackley Brown (Proprietor, Friendly Beauty School)

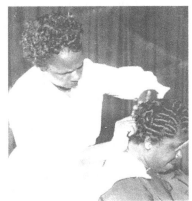

Mamie Mackley Brown's Friendly Beauty School graduated more than two hundred students, who then went on to own and operate beauty and barber shops of their own. Photo courtesy of Aaronita Brown.

After studying at Storer College in Harper's Ferry, West Virginia, and completing training at the Apex School of Cosmetology, Mamie decided to become an entrepreneur. The spark of entrepreneurship was ignited, and she burst onto the business scene as a cosmetologist when she opened her business, The Friendly Beauty Salon in the late 1930s at 2424 South Shirlington Road, in Arlington, Virginia. She later expanded to incorporate a cosmetology school. Her philosophy of "if it's worth doing, it's worth doing right" propelled her to another plateau. Because Virginia did not have a cosmetology board to administer examinations and issue licenses, Mamie's students were provided the opportunity to take the cosmetology examination in the District of Columbia. Friendly's students' high scores on the tests resulted in requests for Mamie to demonstrate her techniques and procedures to other cosmetology schools in the District of Columbia. She served as tutor to prospective candidates preparing to take the board examination. In the early 1960s, she changed the name to Friendly Beautorium because of the expanding services and her intention of relocating to another section of Arlington County. Mrs. Brown held formal graduation ceremonies at the local churches in Arlington, whereas each class selected the church where the students held membership. She graduated well over three hundred students and was pleased to chart the progress of her students as they moved into employment in the cosmetology field. Some students remained operators, while others moved into management or became instructors and owners. More than thirty years after Mamie held the first graduation ceremony at Mount Olive Baptist Church, in Arlington, Virginia, the Commonwealth of Virginia instituted a system of examination. Many Friendly graduates were able to become registered because they held a valid license from the District of Columbia. Mamie Bell Mackley Brown was a woman ahead of her time. Her legacy lives on through her daughters, Alverna and Aaronita, as they have been instilled with her untiring drive throughout their church and community. (Source: Document supplied by daughter, Aaronita Brown)

Richard Walker

If you were African American and your shoes needed repaired, you took them to Mr. Walker. His store was the only shoe repair shop in Arlington that served African Americans. *Photo courtesy of Lloyd Wolfe.*

Kenneth A. (Kenny) Cooper

The late Kenneth A. Cooper began his working career as a shoemaker's apprentice under the leadership of Mr. Moses McCray. Mr. McCray was also his junior Sunday school teacher. In 1959 Mr. Richard Walker was another strong mentor and teacher in trades and allowed him to later open Kenny's Shoe Repair in the Green Valley Community. Kenneth was a long-distance truck driver for Vet Van Lines and the local Giant Food Stores. Later Kenny worked for Arlington County in the Water-Sewer Division, until 1992. As an employee of Arlington County, he assisted the younger individuals in learning their trade. Kenneth was always there to assist in community renovations throughout Arlington County.

He was the son of the late Lloyd and Hattie Cooper. Kenny attended Kemper School and Hoffman-Boston High School. He grew up as a member of Lomax A.M.E. Zion Church. He is the brother of Lloyd (Buddy), Cooper (Martina), Joan Cooper, Iris Cooper McElroy, Dorise Cooper Kenney (Vernon), and Doris Cooper.

Kenny will be remembered for his positive attitude and wonderful personality. His love for his community, friends, family, children, and Pat, and his ever-beautiful smile will forever stay in our hearts and minds. He always repaired our shoes when it was needed, and they'd last forever. We all truly miss him. (Source: Joan E. Cooper, sister)

Elizabeth W. Green

Elizabeth Green, fondly known as Liz, was born on March 28, 1931, in Butler County, Greenville, Alabama. Liz attended public schools in Greenville, Alabama, and graduated from Lomax Hannon College High School. On May 15, 1949, she was joined in holy matrimony to Elbert F. Green, Jr. When they moved to Arlington, she became a member of the Lomax AME Zion Church. Liz was truly a testimony. Her favorite song became her motto in life: "If I Can Help Somebody, My Living Shall Not Be in Vain." Liz was strong. Her strength was a direct source from God; so powerful that it touched everyone she met. She became a licensed beautician and later worked for the Syphax Child Care Center in Arlington, Virginia. The highlight of her industrious career started in 1969 when she became the first State and County licensed home day care provider, until her retirement in June 1988. She received numerous awards for this momentous feat during her life. Graduates and their parents always came back to thank her for her love and support throughout the year. She exemplified strength to everyone she came in contact with, but especially to her family. Each of her children, grandchildren, and adopted children are examples of the strength that she willingly shared.

She was more affectionately known for her dinners, fried fish, chicken, ribs, red velvet cake, apple cobbler, and those melt-in-your-mouth, down-home, gravy-sopping rolls that she and Daddy baked. She welcomed everyone to her table, and anyone who stopped by left full, satisfied, and with an extra plate in their hand to take home. Some folks would often come back the next day, hoping for leftovers. When you came in Liz's house, you walked right upstairs—not to her living room, but to her kitchen—and you sat around the table, listening to her advice and watching television, and you even slept there if you needed to. Her doors were open to all. She fed co-workers, friends, neighbors, county employees, strangers, and her church family. She died on May 5, 1998. (Source: Taken from the obituary program)

Dale Harris

Dale Harris a graduate of Hoffman-Boston, Class of 1964 is President of Bound Brook Ford, located in Bound Brook, New Jersey, a New York City suburb. Bound Brook Ford is a $25 million corporation that was recognized by *Black Enterprise Magazine* for Outstanding Business Achievement and was included as one of the Top 100 most successful African American-owned companies. Dale is also the President of D. F. Harris and Associates, a New York/New Jersey based consulting firm. Dale is the son of the late Richard and Lula Harris, lifelong residents of Nauck and members of St. John's Baptist Church. (Source: 1991 *Green Valley News* article)

George Elliott (Builder)

Housing for African Americans was so scarce that many lived for a time in government-provided trailer parks. When they found vacant land to buy, they hired talented African American craftsmen like George Elliott to build their homes. (Photo courtesy of Gary Barbee)

George and his older brother, John, were born and grew up in Green Valley. Their mother, a nurse in the District, sent John to a trade school to learn to be a carpenter and sent George to learn how to repair shoes. Shoe repair was considered a good occupation for an African American man because it provided a service that everyone needed at one time or another.

With the help of his brother, John, George became a developer. At the time, if an African American family needed a house built they could not hire a white builder to do the work. White builders resisted giving the impression that they were working for African Americans. They were only interested in building large developments for the government or for white developers, not building individual homes for individual African American families. This meant that there was plenty of work for African American builders like the Elliott brothers. They built in all of the African American neighborhoods, including: Johnson's Hill, Halls Hill, and Green Valley.

Like other builders, George needed funding for his building projects, but because he was African American, he could not get building loans at an Arlington bank. He could borrow money from a bank in the District but could not apply money borrowed in the District to a building project in Arlington. Banks are only chartered to loan money in the area where they are located. However, he had become close friends with Edward Smith, a partner at BM Smith and Associates, a large, white-owned real estate and mortgage company in Arlington. There were several mortgage companies in Arlington, but very few would loan money to African Americans. Edward Smith, who studied law in college, was George's biggest cheerleader, encouraging George to expand his business. A lot of George's customers came through BM Smith; the Smith firm financed almost every project that George built. Edward Smith would plan a development that he wanted to have built and then invite George to be the builder. Several other African American builders in Arlington also got some of their funding from BM Smith and Associates.

The Elliott brothers had a reputation as very good builders. They were Class A general contractors, licensed by the State of Virginia. As general contractors, they did not have to hold plumbing licenses or electrical licenses. Those licenses were held by the plumbers or electricians they hired for their projects. The Elliott's subcontracted out any areas of responsibility for which they were not personally licensed. John was licensed to do the framing, and George was licensed to manage the projects, do the grading, and lay the concrete and brick. George was also an excellent plasterer, finishing the interior walls of the new houses.

George lived an exemplary life. He never drank or smoked. He rose early, leaving the house for work before four o'clock in the morning. He expected the same work ethic from his employees. He 'built' his good reputation. He never put up an advertisement sign with his name on it at a building site. He felt that his good word was advertisement enough, and his houses sold themselves. He also surrounded himself with excellent tradesmen, people whose work ethic and standards matched his own. Up through the 1950s, white subcontractors refused to work for an African American contractor, so most of George's subcontractors were African American. However, as Arlington integrated, his workers were of every race. One carpenter was from Sweden. His roofer and his floor layer were white.

After Arlington integrated, George's business expanded. He was no longer limited to building in African American neighborhoods. Edward Smith invited him to build in white neighborhoods, as well as African American neighborhoods. Their friendship worked well for both men. Edward profited from the mortgages on the houses, and George profited because Edward was financing the projects and generating work for George to do.

George remembered his origins. He remembered that his parents were poor, and he strove to pass that on to his children, encouraging them to always live within their means and to work for a living. He never thought of himself as a rich man, so he worked hard up to the day of his death in 1996. George built at least one or two houses every year. He was still building on two houses when he died at seventy-seven years of age. His company closed at his death. None of his children were interested in continuing the business. (Interview of Gary Barbee, son of building contractor George Elliott with Dr. Nancy Perry, July 6, 2010)

Robert and Rupert Baker (Funeral Home Proprietors)

African American mortuaries were guaranteed to have customer because African Americans were unwelcomed in white-owned mortuaries. The Chinn family opened their funeral home in 1946. It is still in operation under the ownership of Robert and Rupert Baker.

Robert B. Baker, Jr.

Robert Bernard Baker, Jr., was born on New Year's Day in 1942. Mr. Baker was raised in Williamsburg, Virginia. At the age of fourteen, Mr. Baker also secured employment at Whiting's Funeral Home. This experience not only reinforced his commitment to give of himself to others, but it also helped him discover his passion for the mortuary sciences and business ownership.

In an effort to fulfill his professional goals, Robert knew that he had to go back to school, so he applied and was invited to attend the Cincinnati College of Mortuary Science. After graduation in 1962, he moved to Hampton, Virginia, to meet his apprenticeship requirements at Cook Brothers Funeral Home. While in Hampton, Mr. Baker's desire to serve his community only intensified and, in 1963, he joined the police department. In doing this, Robert not only courageously came to the aid of others, but he also gained valuable knowledge and exposure to forensics and the laws governing the Commonwealth. He remained in Hampton and dutifully served that city until 1966, when he relocated to Arlington, Virginia. In May 1966, he was employed by James Chinn at Chinn Funeral Service. He was diligent with his work ethic and purchased Chinn Funeral Service in June 1969.

Mr. Baker's care and compassion becomes evident in every interaction he has. Whether it is with a grieving person making funeral arrangements for a loved one or being a source of support for friends and family, he consistently extends himself to those around him. Providing superior funeral services and keeping abreast of any new developments in the industry is also very important to him. To accomplish this, he takes continuing education courses to sharpen his skills, thus solidifying his place among the best in the field. Robert's dedication to excellence does not stop with his professional life. He is also committed to improving his community. Recognizing that Chinn Baker Funeral Service is a staple in the Nauck neighborhood, Robert feels an obligation to lend his time, talent, and finances to support local improvement projects.

In an effort to fulfill this self-proclaimed obligation, Mr. Baker has volunteered to serve on numerous boards and committees. Some of these include holding seats on the Martin Luther King Jr. Teen Center Board, where he served in many different capacities; the Nauck Business Association, where is an elected officer; and the Shirlington Road Revitalization Advisory Board. In addition, Robert is the former treasurer and current president elect for the Northern Virginia District Morticians Association. In addition, he is a member of the Arlington #58 Masonic Lodge.

His hard work and long-standing commitment to his fellow man has not gone unnoticed. Robert Baker has received numerous awards and accolades. These include the prestigious ABBEY Award in 2004 and the Martin Luther King Jr. Appreciation Award almost every year since 1970. He also won the NAACP Community Appreciation Award in 2011. Mr. Baker's acknowledgements aren't limited to neighborhood sources, though. He has been interviewed on the local news as an expert on embalming at the onset of the AIDS epidemic, and he was featured twice in the *Washington Post*. This year he had the honor of being named Mortician of the Year by the Northern Virginia District Morticians Association. The devotion Robert Baker has for community service and helping others has been instrumental in securing Chinn Baker Funeral Service's place in the history of Arlington County. The example he has set through his unwavering commitment to others will undoubtedly continue inspire generations to come.

Rupert B. Baker

Rupert B. Baker, along with his twin brother, Robert, was born on January 1, 1942. He comes from very humble beginnings in rural Williamsburg, Virginia, during an era of segregation and racial inequality. With two, working-class parents, Rupert learned the value of hard work and a solid education. Even as a youngster, he had a heart for giving and a strong sense of responsibility. An example of this is when he worked in a local restaurant during high school to financially assist his parents, while making his own money to take care of his personal needs. In addition to a strong work ethic, a strong sense of loyalty and protectiveness were also qualities given him by his parents. Being one of six children, Mr. Baker had ample opportunities to use his unique skills of persuasion to mediate disputes, discourage bullies, and demonstrate absolute allegiance to his siblings when interacting with peers.

Soon after his eighteenth birthday Mr. Baker made the decision to use his many gifts and talents to serve his country and, in 1960, he joined the United States Air Force. During his tenure in the Air Force he completed tours in Guam, the South Pacific, and Vietnam. He also used his time in the military to educate himself. He graduated from Gunter Air University, majoring in business administration. After six, brave years in the Armed Forces, Rupert received an honorable discharge and relocated to Arlington, Virginia. There he joined his twin brother, Robert, and received his introduction to the funeral business, which he now considers his life's calling.

When he initially moved to Arlington, he worked at Lindsay Cadillac as one of the first African Americans in the parts department. While this was considered steady and reliable employment, Rupert deemed it unfulfilling. After a few years, he found himself having to make the difficult decision to leave his young wife and two-year-old daughter to further his education. Though this was not an easy choice, his dedication to ensuring a good life for his family, loyalty to his brother, and the opportunity to serve his new community in a way he loved made it a necessary one. In 1971 Rupert enrolled in the Cincinnati School for Mortuary Science. While there he looked for ways to positively contribute to his school and fellow students. This ingrained desire to give back to those around him resulted in him being elected the first African American class president in the school's history. After graduating with honors, he returned to his family in Arlington. He also rejoined his brother, and together they worked tirelessly to build Chinn Baker Funeral Services and secure its place as the neighborhood landmark it is today.

In the more than forty years since Rupert Baker has been in Arlington and part of Chinn Baker Funeral Service, he has dedicated himself to making his community a better place. Recognizing that he encounters people during their most difficult times, Rupert tries very hard to ensure their time with him is filled with comfort, professionalism, respect and, at times, a little laughter. The pride he takes in his work mandates that he always goes above and beyond what is required. That is why both he and his brother exhaust all measures to ensure they are always armed with the most up to date advancements for their chosen profession. They do this by enrolling in continuing education classes and attending annual mortuary science conferences and seminars. This desire for excellence is also why the Baker brothers are widely recognized as being among the best in their field. Rupert will tell anyone that his personal philosophy is to always reach out to hurting people and to give to anyone in need. Whether it is offering financial support, emotional comfort, assistance with funeral and estate planning, clothes to wear, food to eat, or place to stay, Mr. Baker is always willing extend himself.

Rupert Baker is also active in many social, civic, and professional organizations. He has been a member of the Arlington #58 Masonic Lodge for many years. He is also an active member of the Northern Virginia District Morticians Association, where he volunteers his time to serve as treasurer and trustee. He was also a trustee for the Virginia Morticians Association. Mr. Baker's hard work and dedication has not gone unnoticed, as he and his brother, Robert, continue to receive countless awards and recognitions annually, including the Arlington County ABBEY Award and various community involvement accolades. Mr. Baker passed away in 2013. (Source: Documents supplied by daughter and niece, Tyra Baker)

Charles E. Collins

African Americans were unwelcome in Arlington Hospital, so Friendly Cab doubled as an ambulance service, taking patients to African American-owned Freedmen's Hospital in Washington, D.C. Friendly Cab is run today by Charles Collins, (pictured), the son of the original owner, Ralph D. Collins, Sr. Photo courtesy of Aaronita Brown.

Charles Collins was born and grew up in Green Valley. He attended elementary school in Green Valley until his family sent him to school in the District; first to Stevens Elementary School, then to Francis Junior High School, and finally to Cardozo High School. He remembered that the schools were crowded. His mother died when he was small, and his grandmother helped raise him. She had a vegetable stand at the K Street Market, right down the street from his school.

Charles' parents were entrepreneurs. Before starting Friendly Cab Company, Charles' father, Ralph D. Collins, Sr., ran a small restaurant on Shirlington Road called Friendly Lunch. His mother ran a beauty shop called Community Beauty, and the family also sold coal in the winter. A lot of African Americans, moving to the Arlington area from the south, came to his father's restaurant in need of a ride. In 1943 he decided that there was need for a cab company, and he started Friendly Cab. This was during World War II when it was hard to buy a car, so the company slowly built their fleet of cabs. At first he had only two cabs, which he bought through two friends of his older sons. The two friends were servicemen; when they came out of the service he asked them to buy cars for him. They did, and that was the beginning of Friendly Cab.

Friendly Cab has always been at its current location, at 3022 South 22nd Street, and was the first African American cab company in Arlington. In 1946 the war ended, and Mr. Collins Sr. was able to purchase two more cabs. In 1964 the company grew to twenty cabs. They could have expanded even more, but they were turned down when they applied for more 'certificates.' Every cab has its own certificate, and the certificates are issued by Arlington County. Charles felt that

Arlington County held Friendly Cab back by refusing to grant them additional certificates. He pointed out that Red Top Cab was not as old as Friendly Cab, but Red Top Cab had five hundred cabs in service in 2010. Finally, in 2007, Friendly Cab was granted seven more certificates, and in 2012 they received twelve more certificates.

From 1958 until 1973, Friendly Cab was able to offer two-way radio service. This made it possible for a passenger to call the company from wherever they were, and the dispatcher could notify a driver to get the passenger. There were also direct-line boxes in grocery stores, shelters, and other locations. The customer could call the cab company directly from the box to request a ride. The problem was that the company had too few cabs for the amount of business. Passengers called to ask for a ride, but there were no available cabs to come pick them up. Friendly Cab gave up the boxes and the two-way radio service capability, and the drivers limited themselves to waiting at taxi stands at the airport and at certain hotels and motels to pick up their fares. The biggest motel they covered was the Marriott Twin Bridges Motel. Friendly Cab had the latest-model cars and did a good business, giving rides to both African American and white passengers. This was during Segregation, when white-owned cab companies would not hire an African American driver, so Friendly Cab benefitted from this. Some of their best drivers were off-duty African American firemen. Who can find an address better than a fireman? Nowadays most of the Friendly Cab drivers are Asians and Africans.

Friendly Cab provides a service to the public schools by driving wheelchair-bound children to and from school. They were the only small cab company that had vehicles equipped to handle a wheelchair. They also provide rides to the elderly to doctor appointments, using a vehicle that has no signs on it to indicate that it is a cab. Charles referred to that as the 'sedan' service.

Charles said his father had no difficulty purchasing cars when he needed them. He was friends with the sheriff, who owned a car dealership in Ballston. So when he bought a new cab, he got it from the sheriff. He had so many African American and white friends in Arlington that even during Segregation he was able to get the cooperation of the County when he needed something, whether it was licenses for his restaurant or licenses for his wife's beauty shop. The only difficulty his father had, that Charles remembered, was getting additional cab certificates.

While he was still in school, Charles worked for his father at the Friendly Cab Company. He felt that the best year for Friendly Cab was around 1954. The population in the County was growing rapidly as the Federal Government dispersed out of the District, many apartment buildings and motels were going up, and people needed a ride. One of the hot spots for Friendly Cab was Shirlington. Most of the customers were white rather than were African American. It was not by accident that their business was so good during this period as Friendly Cab advertised. Everybody who moved to Arlington received a letter from the company telling them about Friendly Cab. Even President Richard Nixon lived at one time in Arlington and received one of their letters.

Charles described two kinds of customers that Friendly Cab had: wealthy businessmen who didn't want to bother to drive themselves, and poor people who could not afford a car. Charles described the poor customers as needing a ride when they went to do laundry or get groceries. That business was especially brisk on Saturdays. He said they seldom drive people to and from the grocery or laundry any more now that the STARR cabs are available. Friendly Cab never took part in the STARR program. (Interview with Dr. Nancy Perry, July 15, 2010.)

Charles also worked as a supervisor at Arlington County Solid Waste Division for many years. He passed away in August of 2013. He left behind a daughter and two sons.

George Moore (Founder and Proprietor of Naomi's T.V. Repair)

African Americans had to carry their T.V.s to Washington, D.C. to be repaired, so George Moore opened Naomi's T.V. Repair Services in order to save them the trip. Mr. Moore is still in business.

George Moore is a native of Barbados, arriving in Arlington in 1944 when he was nineteen years old. George attended trade schools in the District and in New York. When he arrived, Arlington was very segregated. African Americans were limited in where they could live, eat, shop, and go to school. George remembered the constraints that segregation imposed on African Americans, but still he made some good friends who were white. He explained that segregation was as scary for friendly whites as it was for African Americans. Whites were afraid to be seen being kind to an African American person, so friendships had to be conducted carefully.

George is the owner of Naomi's T.V. Repair Shop. He got his start in the T.V. repair business because of segregation. There was a white-owned T.V. repair shop in nearby Shirlington, and George had a T.V. that needed to be repaired, so he took it to the Shirlington shop. There was also a T.V. repair shop in Georgetown. In those days, T.V. sets were much bigger and heavier than they are today, so carrying the T.V. to the shop required a real effort. The Shirlington shop owner made George wait around for service and then told him he did not have time to wait on George that day and to come back down with his T.V. again the next week. This answer did not make George happy! He decided he would learn how to repair T.V.s himself. He went to a T.V. repair school in New York, learned the trade, and returned to Arlington.

Until George could build his own repair shop, he worked as a traveling serviceman for RCA, getting calls from customers who had broken T.V. sets, making house calls to do the repair work and bringing his tools with him. His customers were African American and white. They didn't care what race George was—just that he did what he said he would do, that he serviced their T.V. set correctly, and that he charged a fair price. George earned many loyal customers during this period.

George wanted to build a T.V. repair shop in Green Valley. He already owned a lot on Shirlington Road, which had a record business called D Record Den with an apartment above where George and his family lived. He wanted to tear the building down and replace it with a T.V. repair shop, with a couple of apartments above. He went to the Old Dominion Bank for a loan. The bank was willing to give him a car loan so he could buy a Lincoln or a Cadillac, but not a loan to build a T.V. repair shop. George realized that he would have to get a private loan from someone who had money to lend because the bank was not going to do business with him. He understood that in order for people to trust him enough to loan him the money for his new shop, he needed to treat them with respect, to dress nicely, to treat them the way he would want to be treated himself, and to be very businesslike. One white friend realized that George needed a loan to build his repair shop. He told George one day that he would make him the loan, but that George must be totally honest with him, and George must promise to tell no one who lent him the money. George agreed, borrowed the money, built his business, and paid the money back regularly until the loan was cleared. He remained friends with that man for many years.

When the Vietnam War ended in the 1970s, and migrants were coming to Arlington from Laos, Viet Nam, and Cambodia, George borrowed five hundred dollars from this friend to buy rice for a group of Southeast Asian immigrants. George remembered how people helped him in the past when he needed it, and he wanted to do the same for these people in need. He rented a truck, drove up to New York City, and brought back fifty, one hundred-pound bags of rice for his new immigrant friends. He is still friends with the immigrants; one of them is his godchild. They have remained in contact with George, visiting him and he visiting them. They have never forgotten his kindness.

Once George built his own T.V. repair shop, he earned a loyal following. Even after Arlington became integrated and African Americans could take their T.V. sets to white-owned repair shops, most of his old customers remained loyal to him. In addition to offering good service at a reasonable price, George offered something the white-owned repair shops did not offer: He allowed his customers to pay their bill on time if they could not afford to pay the entire bill at one time. As of 2010, George was still working at Naomi's T.V. Repair. Since Green Valley has become more integrated, particularly with more Hispanic residents, George's customers have also become more integrated. He said that he has had to learn to speak a little Spanish to deal with his Hispanic customers. The land where George's shop sits has become very valuable over the years. Many individuals have tried to convince him to sell it. So far he has resisted moving.

George was not only a successful T.V. repairman; he was also a successful father. His sons attended high school in Arlington after the schools were integrated, and they graduated from Wakefield High School. One of his sons went to college and both his sons are doing very well. He plans to leave them his business when he dies if they want it. (Interview with Dr. Nancy Perry, July 15, 2010)

Marie A. Mosby (Infant/Child Care)

Marie A. Mosby (Ms. P-Nut's House LLC), is a licensed home infant/child care provider in Arlington, Virginia, looking to expand to accommodate the large influx of children in the immediate area. She chose to open an infant/child care business as a new career because she loves children and loves the idea of being home and starting a new and more rewarding work experience. She is currently licensed in Arlington and the State of Virginia for nine children, at maximum capacity. She is the oldest of six children and among the oldest of a large, extended family. At an early age, she provided child care for her siblings and other neighboring children. She raised one child.

She retired from a large technology company and found that she was still energetic enough to do many things, which include volunteer work in her community involving children. She is a lifelong resident of Arlington County, and attended public schools in Virginia. She obtained a Master's degree from George Washington University, a Masters certification from the Stevens Institute of Technology, and she spent over thirty-five years working in private industry, mainly telecom. She started her own consulting business, contracting telecom internationally for over five years. She has traveled to, and lived in, countries around the world as part of jobs contracted to develop telecommunications systems in technologically emerging countries. She is a certified Al's Caring Pals Trainer and President of the Virginia Alliance of Family Child Care Associations (VirginiaFCCA). She worked as a volunteer for the Arlington County Office on Aging for twenty-four years in the Guardianship Program and received an AARP national award of recognition for volunteerism.

Currently she has a child certificate in Infant and Toddler Programs and an Associate of Applied Science degree in Early Childhood Development Child, an asset to her line of work. Ms. P-NUT's HOUSE LLC got its name from a nickname of "Peanut" given to her by her uncle. Upon returning home from the war, seeing her as a baby for the first time, he declared that she was only peanut-size and thus the nickname was born. It has followed her throughout her entire life; even today everyone calls her Ms. P, Auntie P, or a version of the peanut name.

She offers lots of love, patience, respect, and care for children. Her goal and objective is to provide the same type of environment that her child was able to enjoy. She treats each child as if he/she were her own. She is Infant/Child-CPR trained, medical administration-trained(MAT), First Aid-certified, and she loves to cook, play on the computer, and garden. (She has over one hundred blooming plants and trees around her home.) Her business is operating successfully in Arlington, Virginia. (Source: Marie Mosby)

Verna Lee (Taylor) Dean

Little has changed in the tiny, white house on the grassy slope in the Green Valley area of Arlington since Mamma Dean died last week. School children still play in its blossom-lined backyard, where generations tested their young muscles and nerve in childhood adventures. Children's photographs still fill living room table tops, and during thunderstorms, the house still grows quiet so its inhabitants can hear the sound of "God's work."

But the home at 2110 South Kenmore Street is now without seventy-four-year-old Verna Lee Dean, the woman who set its rhythms in motion. For almost half a century, Mamma Dean, as she was called by nearly everyone who knew her, had been a surrogate mother to thousands of children, church, and community leaders. She was a self-appointed social worker who provided low-cost or free day care for generations of working parents, long before government agencies began during the same.

She also raised one, natural daughter; five, adopted daughters; five children from her husband's previous marriage; and dozens of informally adopted children brought to her by parents unable to care for their infants. Even government social service agencies, after years of asking her to get the required license for her work, eventually caved in to this one-woman institution and began sending her foster children.

"She was a bank, a marriage counselor, and a career counselor," said Mike Scott, twenty-one, who Dean raised as her son. "When she spoke, people listened. What she said, you could count on."

So when Mrs. Dean died suddenly of a respiratory condition, it was no surprise that the Macedonia Baptist Church was crowded with nearly three hundred people, many of whom were in no small sense her sons, daughters, grandchildren, and great-grandchildren.

It started forty-seven years ago, when Verna Lee Dean found herself unexpectedly without an escort for a church dinner. Deacon Henry Dean became a late substitute, and in short order, the two were married. Her husband, now ninety-two, survives her.

The new Mrs. Dean immediately became the mother of five children from her husband's previous marriage. But the five would not be enough for Mrs. Dean, who worked regularly in church and did sewing and domestic work when she could find it near her Arlington home, while her husband worked construction.

Two years after the Deans were married, a next-door neighbor had a baby girl. "That was me," Edna Taylor, forty-five, said, with a chuckle. "I was three months old when my mother got too sick to take care of me." Mrs. Dean offered to take care of her until her natural mother became strong enough to do it herself. But Taylor said she came to be spoiled on Mrs. Dean's kindness and never returned to her natural mother. That set the pattern for many similar adoptions to come.

"I've always said I had two mothers and two fathers," Taylor said. "I thought it was a blessing from God."

Life in the Dean household was a careful balance of reward and reward, her children joke. Scott said he remembers Mrs. Dean's dinner tables of meatloaf, ham, salad, stewed tomatoes, sweet corn, and cakes. "It was something," Scott said. "You know how she used to find out if you had enough? She would keep putting food on your plate until you left something."

And because there were often twenty-five to thirty children in her home at lunchtime, Scott said Mrs. Dean taught all her charges, out of necessity, how to share and be considerate of each other.

"You just didn't have any trouble, not in Mamma Dean's home," Scott said. "She would come out and tell us, 'Lunch is ready,' and without saying another word, we knew to line up to wash our hands and take our places at the table."

Taylor said the girls took turns washing the dishes, and the boys did work on the house and in the yard. When the fresh vegetable truck pulled up twice a week, the boys, from toddlers to teenagers, pitched in to carry in what they could. That was Mrs. Dean's method, her children said.

Anne Dean Workman, thirty-three, is Mrs. Dean's only natural daughter. She said she doesn't know why her mother didn't have any other children of her own, but she always thought of her house full of children as normal, as if she simply had more than the usual number of brothers and sisters. Throughout the day, waves of children would come and go, as parents came at all hours to retrieve their sons and daughters after a day or night of work, a completed semester at high school or college, or a decade or so after regaining control of a fallen life. Her children said they never heard Mrs. Dean say an ill word about their natural parents. She was never judgmental. "You know everybody who grew up in Mamma Dean's home didn't turn out to be saints," said Scott, a clean-cut looking musician and technician for a local rock band. Some of them went wrong, went to jail, or became alcoholics.

"But Mamma Dean could never say no," Scott said. If they didn't have a place to go, she'd take them in. She'd feed them, She'd lend them money."

"She was always understanding," Workman said. "She has always been a lover of children and a lover of people. She said nothing ever happened without a reason. She was a Christian woman inspired by God."

At her funeral this week, Reverend Clarence A. Robinson, pastor of Macedonia Baptist Church where Mrs. Dean sang in the senior choir and was a member of a half a dozen groups, said Mrs. Dean conquered misfortunes that would have overloaded other people.

In mid-1969, Jay Dial, then sixteen, and one of the children she kept for years while his parents worked, was walking in Dean's neighborhood when someone in a passing car shot him, Scott said. Badly wounded, Dial ran to the Dean home, where he collapsed and died on her porch. "It broke her heart," Scott recalled, adding that the murder was never solved.

"She had the steps torn down." Workman said her mother asked her husband to build new steps because she kept imagining the imprint of Dial's body. "She said, 'You can't wash away murder blood,'" Workman said.

Several years ago, the children of one of her nieces staying with her at the time bolted into the street and were struck and killed by a truck. Scott said some of the neighborhood children threatened to stop taking their children to her. But the practice had become ingrained over the generations. They kept coming—children of children she had kept in her household.

"She inspired many people in her lifetime by the things people saw her do," said Toni Bragg, a longtime friend of the family. "Even though she's gone, people think to themselves, 'How can I carry on her tradition?' But if they knew her, they'd know."

A social worker for Arlington County's Department of Human Resources said although Mrs. Dean was never licensed, the department recognized her home as a good place to put children and therefore sometimes sent children there. In fact, shortly before Mrs. Dean's death, DHR had recommended that two more foster children be sent to her.

John Robinson, director of the Martin Luther King, Jr. Community Center, which provides social and employment services for the area, said some parents don't know who will care for their children now.

"They know she served a purpose no one else would do, taking care of the forgotten children," Robinson said. "Giving them a good, clean home where there was caring. Now that she's gone, it's going to be a problem." *(Source: Friday, June 1, 1982, Washington Post)*

Lena Lachelle "Shelly" Baker-Scott

Lena Lachelle Baker-Scott was born on October 20, 1969, to her parents, Rupert and Sallie Baker. She was named after her paternal grandmother, Lena Baker, who nicknamed her "Shelly." Shelly was raised in south Arlington and attended Oakridge and Claremont Elementary Schools, Kenmore Intermediate School, and she graduated from Yorktown High School in 1987. During her tenure in the Arlington County Public School System, Shelly joined many clubs and organizations, ranging from DECCA and Future Business Leaders of America to managing the junior varsity boys basketball team and the Spanish club. Both of her parents valued education and stressed the importance of always striving to do well academically. They both sacrificed their time, finances, and other resources so that she could make the most of her education, all while instilling in her the confidence that she could reach any goal she set for herself. This education and her parents unwavering support and belief in her potential gave her the necessary foundation to go on to achieve her higher education goals. She attended Howard University from 1987 to 1991, majoring in psychology. After receiving her undergraduate degree, she went on to earn two masters degrees, one in psychology and the other in social work, in 2005 and 2013, respectively.

She spent her entire childhood immersed in the Nauck community. Most of her days growing up were spent at Chinn/Baker Funeral Services, a family-owned business, where her father, Rupert Baker, Director, and her Uncle Robert Baker, Owner, worked tirelessly to service the funeral needs of grieving families in the Nauck and surrounding areas with care, compassion, dedication, and excellence. While there she also learned the value of working hard, the power of community, the importance of family, and the inherent responsibility we each have to give back to those who are less fortunate.

This commitment to excellence and serving others was so deeply engrained in Shelly that she decided, like her father and uncle, to dedicate her life to meeting the needs of hurting people. Though her calling was not to follow in her family's footsteps and go into the funeral business, her path led her to meet her community's mental health needs. Being raised to see value in everyone, Mrs. Baker-Scott decided to make addictions counseling and sex offender treatment her clinical specialty areas, as she was naturally drawn to the client population that many mental health professionals and society as a whole dismissed.

In order to achieve her professional goals, Shelly Baker-Scott left her beloved Nauck community and, in 1994, she moved to Hampton, Virginia. There she attended graduate school, gained her first experiences working with individuals with mental health diagnoses, and discovered her passion for advocacy and entrepreneurship. She also made the decision to marry and start a family. On September 3, 1997, she married Corey Scott and shortly thereafter gave birth to their daughter, Cameryn Parish Scott.

While her family was still young, Shelly Baker-Scott made the bold move start her own business. This decision came from feeling discouraged and undervalued in the work place, so in 2000, she and two friends opened Agape Counseling & Therapeutic Services, Inc. (ACTS). ACTS is a community based mental health agency that is aimed at being employee-friendly while providing an array of outstanding mental health counseling services to at-risk youth and their families, adults with intellectual disabilities and/or mental illnesses, individuals suffering from addictions, sex offenders, victims of violence, and those experiencing grief and loss. The goal of ACTS is to preserve and strengthen our community through the provision of psychological services, thus reducing the risk of out-of-home placement, such as foster care for juveniles, incarceration, and/or hospitalization. In the years since its inception, ACTS has grown from having three employees to over three hundred and has seven, regional offices throughout the State of Virginia.

In addition to starting ACTS, Shelly Baker-Scott and her business partners created a non-profit agency called Agape Foundation, Inc., which attempts to meet the more tangible and/or physical needs that a person or family may, have such as providing food baskets on Christmas, Thanksgiving, and Easter, sponsoring school supply drives throughout Virginia, and offering free tutoring and mentoring services to youth. Mrs. Baker-Scott, through her foundation, has also instituted a clothing closet designed to help students with back-to-school clothes and adults with proper job-seeking and inter-viewing attire. Agape Foundation, Inc. is also responsible for supporting the Rupert B. Baker and James E. Porter Agape Café, which feeds hungry children and their families healthy and nutritious food in a nurturing and uplifting environment. The café's motto is: "Expanding a person's palate expands their world."

In 2010 Shelly Baker-Scott co-founded Mawusi Scott properties, which acquires, renovates, and manages commer-cial and residential real estate throughout Virginia. She is also a full partner in Kids and Books Academy, an educational childcare center that emphasizes the importance of reading by instilling a love of books beginning in infancy. The goal of Kids and Books Academy is to stimulate learning and brain development by fostering a child's natural curiosity through the steady exposure to hearing and seeing the written word as early as six weeks old.

Shelly Baker-Scott also has served on many state and local committees that are focused on improving the access to mental health services for Virginia residents, such as the Peninsula Human Rights Committee, the City of Chesapeake Youth Council, The Peninsula Attention Deficit and Disabilities Association, and Equipping Businesses For Success Institute. She is also a member of the Hampton Newport News Chapter of CHUMS, Inc., which is a civic organization that provides female mentors to adolescent girls who are affiliated with the local Department of Social Services and actively sponsors fundraising events to raise monies for college scholarships for local students. Mrs. Baker-Scott is also an active member of the Hampton Alumnae Chapter of Delta Sigma Theta Sorority Incorporated. (Source: Shelly Baker-Scott)

Community Activists

Lillian Beatrice Bullock Green
James E. Boger
Milton Isiah Rowe, Sr.
Audrey Annette Taylor Coachman
Aaronita Estelle Mackley Brown
Dr. Shakina Dunbar Rawlings
Ernest E. Johnson
Edward D. Strother
Solomon H. Thompson
Alice Strother
Res. Henry H. Sink
Reverend Sherman W. Phillips
Anne P. Belcher
Jenny Davis
John Robinson, Jr.
Thaddenia Hayes West
Portia Clark
Vivian Bullock
Pauline Johnson Ferguson
Robert (Bob) Winkler
Joan E. Cooper
LaVerne Roberts Langhorne
Kimberly M. Roberts
Yolanda Johnson Black
Esther Georgia Irving Cooper

Lillian Beatrice Bullock Green

Lillian Green was born on March 19, 1912, in Arlington, Virginia and passed away on November 6, 2012. She was the third child of the late Thomas and Mary Belle Bullock's four children. Her siblings were Stephen Bullock, Granderson Bullock and Evelyn Bullock Simms. On October 23, 1932, Lillian and Richard Green were married. They had four children: Reverend Richard O. Green, Sr., George A. Green, Gloria A. Taylor, and Gwendolyn E. Stanford. She was very proud of her many grand, great-grand, and great-great-grandchildren.

Mrs. Green attended Kemper Elementary School through eighth grade. Since there were no high schools for African American students in Arlington County, she graduated from Armstrong High School in Washington, D.C. As a young person, Mrs. Green memorized and performed dramatic poetry recitations in several churches and schools throughout the D.C. Metro area, including Lomax A.M.E. Zion Church, where she was a lifetime member.

Mrs. Green worked in government service and was an insurance agent and a newspaper reporter. She was also secretary for the Veterans Memorial Y.M.C.A., where she served as the interim youth coordinator. She retired from the Arlington County School system, where she worked for many years as secretary to Drew Elementary School.

Mrs. Green was an outstanding and respected citizen of Arlington County, and she remained an involved, loyal, and concerned resident throughout her life. For her, social change and making life better for others—particularly African Americans—was always important. She organized the first African American Girl Scout and Brownie troops in South Arlington in the 1940s and was instrumental in establishing other troops. This was novel and historic for an African American woman at that time. As a result, many young, African American girls were afforded opportunities to attend numerous activities with other scouts, such as the Boy Scout Jamboree at Fort Meyer. Arlington County also sent her to a national scouts meeting for a week of training at Camp Macy in Upper New York, where she was the only black person participating. Her troop met at her home and strictly followed the Girl Scout Promise. Despite racial discrimination, her troop was able to function just like other Girl Scout troops. Their activities included visiting the White House and other historical sites, hiking, biking, camping, creating useful crafts, and performing community service, such as delivering fruit to patients at Freedmen's Hospital.

Mrs. Green worked hard, during the struggles of this nation, for ideals that would affect not only African Americans, but all Americans. She was among those who were determined to see that everyone had equal access to a good education. As an active member of the P.T.A. at Kemper School and Hoffman-Boston High School, she played a leadership role in petitioning the County School Board for a complete library and for the high school to be accredited. Her appreciation for an accredited high school was deepened because there were no high schools available for African American children in the area when she completed elementary school. In the 1950s, her son, Reverend Richard O. Green, was denied the right to an education in automobile mechanics in Arlington County School System because the program was only available at the whites-only Washington-Lee High School. Through a court petition and the efforts of Mrs. Green and the NAACP, he was finally admitted to the school. After graduating and completing a tour of duty in the Army, her son was offered and accepted a teaching position in the auto shop of the same school and taught there for several years.

Voting was always a serious issue for Mrs. Green. Her keen interest in all things pertaining to community and country were so evident as she cast her vote, proudly signing her absentee ballot in support of the first African American to become President of the United States of America, and later, to support him in his second term.

The Martin Luther King, Jr. Center, the Arlington Branch of the NAACP, Lomax A.M.E. Zion Church, the Jolly Hearts, and others in the Nauck Community recognized her over the years for her steadfast work on behalf of those in need of physical, economic, spiritual, social, and community support. Mrs. Green was a role model for family, friends, and many who knew and loved her. She had a kind and giving spirit and a winning smile that inspired others to strive to achieve greater things. She lived her life to the fullest, and her journey leaves a legacy of being a renaissance woman for whom few challenges were too great. (Source: Gwendolyn Stanford, daughter)

James E. Boger

James E. Boger was a native of Concord, North Carolina. He graduated from Livingstone College, Class of 1932, in Salisbury, North Carolina. He was chosen by the college to be an Alumni Affairs class agent. Mr. Boger began graduate work at Iowa State University. After teaching history and social studies in Cabarrus County, North Carolina, for eleven years, Mr. Boger moved to Washington, D.C. and gained employment with the Army Corps of Engineers in 1956 for many years. He later served as employment counselor for the United Planning Organization, USES, and finally as senior caseworker with the U.S. Department of Labor, retiring in 1979. His last teaching position was at Lorton Reformatory, in Lorton, Virginia.

He enjoyed playing both football and basketball for several years in his prime. He was moved into a coaching position after a serious leg injury. In addition, he often spoke about his interaction with President Franklin D. Roosevelt and especially with Mrs. Eleanor Roosevelt. Also one of the greatest and exciting times in his life was having the opportunity to become acquainted with Booker T. Washington on the Livingstone College campus.

During the 1970s, Mr. Boger became a Boy Scout executive under the aegis of the Christian Education Department, which was headquartered initially at Metropolitan Wesley AME Zion Church in Washington, D.C. He spearheaded the Arlington Scouts, where he counseled and trained youth throughout the Washington Metropolitan area. His travels to Scout jamborees and related activities for the next fifteen years kept the young people encouraged toward a purposeful career in life.

Mr. Boger went to Johannesburg, South Africa, in 1994 to celebrate the upcoming Mandela Presidency as part of the Arthur Fletcher and Constance B. Newman delegation. He rejoiced day and night during this meaningful trip. "This is just the beginning!" he would repeatedly say after that Conference, according to his brother-in-law, Dr. Leslie Anderson, who also accompanied him to South Africa. Months later he began planning for yet another humanitarian journey with Dr. Anderson's entourage that took him to Utrecht, Netherlands; Switzerland; Austria; England; Germany; Italy; and France in the summer of 1995.

Mr. Boger was a member of Lomax AME Zion Church in Arlington, Virginia, and the United Methodist Men. He was a staunch supporter of the Democratic National Committee; a member of the Coalition for Desert Storm; President Clinton's Saxophone Club; the Founder's Registry of the FDR Memorial; and Habitat for Humanity. He was a member of the Arlington Community Action Program (ACAP) and was always willing to volunteer in the community where he spent forty years. He was married to Renata Anderson Boger. (Source: Obituary)

Milton Isiah Rowe, Sr.

Milton Rowe, Sr. was born on November 7, 1925, in Washington, D.C. He is the great-grandson of William Augustus Rowe, who was the overseer of Freedmen's Village, which was located in Arlington Cemetery. William Augustus Rowe, whose portrait hangs in the Arlington County Central Library, became the first African American to serve as Chairman of the Arlington County Board of Supervisors in the 1870s. Milton is a lifelong, vibrant resident of the Nauck community and was educated in the Arlington County and Washington, D.C. Public Schools. During World War II, he served in the United States Coast Guard on the U.S.S. Pocatello.

He married Ruth M. Robinson (deceased) of Staunton, Virginia, at Lomax AME Zion Church in 1945. He is the father of four children, eleven grandchildren, nine great-grandchildren, one daughter-in-law, and one son-in-law. He is a devoted father. On a plaque (located at South Shirlington Road and South Four Mile Run Drive) marking the historical site of the former Paul Lawrence Dunbar Homes, Ruth and Milton are cited as original owners of housing built for veterans returning from the war (World War II). He is a lifelong member of the Lomax AME Zion Church, where he served in the following capacities: Junior and Senior Trustee Boards, Steward Board, Building Fund Committee, Banquet and Catering Committees, and other projects and programs, as needed. Lomax has recognized and honored him several times.

After thirty-seven years of employment at the Pentagon (Department of the Army), he retired in 1981. He was a dedicated "family man" and, while raising his four kids, he always worked second jobs to provide for them. He became a professional "butler," serving his own clientele with other butlers on their bookings and working for catering firms. As such, this engaged him in the Washington social scene, working bar mitzvahs, weddings, and private parties at embassies and in the homes of politicians. He met George H. W. Bush before he became President. He often worked at the home of Robert F. Kennedy in McLean, Virginia, where he met President John F. Kennedy, to whom he loaned his boots on an occasion. Later he worked at the White House on the Butler's Special Event staff, including State dinners from the Reagan to the Clinton years and has photos with all of them. He has a full-page photo in Hillary Clinton's White House Memories Book.

He has always been active in community, civic, religious, and service organizations. To name a few: Advisor to Boy Scout Troop 589 of Arlington, Virginia (1950s and 1980s); the Butler's Club of Washington, D.C.; Nauck Civic Association; Arlington Housing Committee; NAACP; and the YMCA (Charter member of the Veterans Memorial Y's Men's Club). He presently serves as the Sergeant-at-Arms of the American Legion's Dorie Miller Post 194, in Arlington, Virginia; The Jolly Hearts Club; a Dining Out Group; and several other senior citizen groups. He also pursues an active hobby and interest agenda, including: family historian, researcher of ancestries, reader of documentaries (non-fiction) on slavery, searching the Internet, fishing, traveling, and music (jazz, blues, and gospel). (Source: Milton Isiah Rowe, Sr.)

Audrey Annette (Taylor) Coachman

Audrey Coachman was born on March 12, 1932, to the late Alfred O. and Ruby L. Taylor in Arlington, Virginia. She was blessed with one brother, Alfred O. Taylor Jr., to whom she was devoted. Her early education was acquired at Kemper Elementary School in Arlington, Virginia, and Francis Junior High in Washington, D.C. She graduated from the District of Columbia's Cardozo High School in 1950.

While a student at Cardozo, Audrey met the love of her life. Her marriage to the late Ira Walter Coachman was blessed with three daughters: Jacqueline, Arlene (Kent), and Marcia (Charles). The union was further blessed with grandchildren, André and Vanessa Chapman and Portia (Aaron) and Terri Smith. The role she likely enjoyed most was that of great-grandmother to Skyler Chapman-Maus, Ra'Sheila, DáJee, and Aaron Smith II. The fact that he was born on her birthday is just one reason for her special relationship with her nephew, Kenny Taylor. Among those who will miss her deeply are her niece, Karen; her sisters-in-law Etha Brooks, Juanita Coachman, and Dorothy Coachman; her friends Estelle Williamson and Clara Lamback; and a host of cousins, nieces, nephews, and friends. She was predeceased by a son-in-law, Ivy Chapman; sisters-in-law Oniza Culver, Alzenia Mitchell, Leola Coleman, Margaret Koonce, Emolious Lewis, and Eureka Joyner; and brothers-in-law Garner Coachman, Gertha Coachman, Isaac Brooks, and Arnett Mitchell.

Audrey was a child when she dedicated herself to Christ and joined Macedonia Baptist Church. Her lifetime of service began as pianist for the junior and senior choirs. Examples of over seventy years of constant and unfailing dedication to the Christian obligation of service included: coordinator of the Forerunners Ministry and member of the March Birthday Club, the Recreation Ministry, and the Chair of the Deaconess Ministry.

Her past employment and retirement as a data librarian at Control Data was a testament to her devotion to duty and a legacy of reliability. Never one to rest on her laurels, upon retiring, Audrey immediately began her service to Alexandria City Public Schools as coordinator of the system that scheduled substitute teachers. Although she left that position years ago, many still speak of her with affection and admiration.

Audrey expanded her commitment to service beyond her church, family, and career. She was an avid bowler for decades and enjoyed the fellowship of the Tuesday morning bowling league. A founding member of Jolly Hearts, the senior citizens club blossomed under her leadership and support. Because of her service to Jolly Hearts, she was appointed to an advisory committee on senior citizen initiatives that was convened by Arlington County Government. The seniors and homebound in South Arlington who knew her because of her volunteer work with Meals on Wheels were especially appreciative of her dedication to the motto: "service with a smile." There are literally hundreds who looked forward to the greeting cards they knew they would receive at least once a year. Many have commented that they could always count on her to remember their birthday. When she was not blessing others with her generosity and sweet spirit, she enjoyed traveling with her beloved brother, sister-in-law, and cousin, Emily. (Source: Obituary)

Aaronita Estelle Mackley Brown

Aaronita Brown is the second oldest daughter of the late Reverend Dr. Aaron Mackley and Deaconess Mamie Mackley Brown. Although she was born and raised in Washington, D.C., she has resided primarily in Arlington, Virginia. She attended Kemper School, Drew Elementary, Shaw Junior High, Cardozo Senior High, Miners Teachers College, D.C., the University of the District of Columbia, and Evans Smith Institute in Virginia Union.

Although widowed in Jan 1966 from her sweetheart, the late Carlton J. Brown, Sr., this marriage of eleven years bore two children, Carlton J. Brown, Jr. and Gwendolyn D. Brown. Ms. Brown began attending Mt. Pleasant in 1964 and later joined in 1966. Initially she served as assistant to the Sunday school choir, assistant to the junior choir, and later, in 1969, organized and became the coordinator of the first youth choir. Throughout the years, she has been a dedicated vocalist for the following choirs: senior choir (thirty-three years), Evangelistic Outreach Choir, Baltimore Specials, Mass Choir, and the Voices. She also was a member of the Interdenominational Ushers Chorus of Virginia during the sixties and seventies.

She has served as a member of the Board of Christian Education from 1972 to 1999. She served as assistant superintendent of the Church School from 1968 to 1974. From 1974 until the present, Ms. Brown has served as director of the Church School. Under her leadership, the following accomplishments were made: the Church School van was purchased and put into operation in October 1986; five, new classes were started, which included the Young Adults,

Young Pioneers, Intermediate Adults, Preteens, and Middlers; the library was completed under her leadership, with shelving and new books; and the Sunday school was renamed under her leadership to Church School, so that it would reflect the entire family.

Her involvement with the Church School led her to become a member of the Fairfax Central Baptist Sunday School Union, where she served as the second vice president and later president. She also served as statistical secretary of the Baptist Sunday school and the Baptist Training Union Congress of Virginia, and presently as a field worker.

Ms. Brown has served on the anniversary, youth, and other varied committees; she currently serves with the Homeless Ministry, Mount Pleasant's Budget Committee and is a van driver. She has received numerous awards and plaques and has continued her studies in Christian education, taking over seven hundred courses in the last thirty years.

Finally, she is a Golden Lifetime Member of the NAACP, Lifetime Member of the Fairfax Central Baptist Sunday School Union (formally serving as the president for eleven years) and the Northern Virginia Baptist Sunday school and the B.T.U. Convention, and Lifetime Member of the Baptist Sunday school and the Baptist Training Union Congress of Virginia. She presently serves as first vice president over all of the Sunday schools in Virginia and as the field worker for The Baptist Sunday school and the Baptist Training Union Congress of Virginia.

Her faith in God and God's Word has brought her through many trying situations. One of her favorite scriptures is Psalm 121: "I will lift up mine eyes unto the hills from whence cometh my help, my help cometh from the Lord."

Ms. Brown retired from Arlington Public Schools on January 31, 1996, after serving as an assistant to the principal for thirty-one years. Previously she had many other jobs, such as teacher's aide, janitor at Mt. Pleasant, grocery store clerk, babysitter, short-order cook, and house cleaner, and she worked at the Drug Fair Drug stores, the Green Valley Pharmacy, and Friendly Beauty School, where she received her license as a cosmetologist. She says "she has always had to do what she had to do to make ends meet."

In her spare time, she enjoys sports (especially football), bowling, fishing, family, cooking, camping, and traveling. She has seen most of the United States and has cruised to many islands. She has always loved children, and her first volunteer job was at the Northwest Settlement House, a home for under privileged children.

Her extended family consisted of her late godson (Edward "Pete" Green), who she raised from the age of thirteen until he joined the military; two other godsons, now deceased (Buddy Wallace and Freddie Davis); three goddaughters (Shericka Parks, Shantice Bates, and Tameka Davis); and two, adopted daughters: Ruby Mate-Kole, residing in Accra, Ghana; and Janine Carter, residing in Clinton, Maryland. (Source: Aaronita Brown)

Dr. Shakina D. Rawlings

Shakina Dunbar Rawlings is a native of Arlington, Virginia. Dr. Rawlings holds a Bachelor of Arts degree in Sociology from George Mason University, a Master of Divinity degree from Howard University School of Divinity, and an earned Doctorate of Ministry Degree in Prophetic Preaching for the 21st Century from the United Theological Seminary. Dr. Rawlings dissertation work was entitled, "Prophetic Preaching that Transforms the Leadership Structure and Development of the Church."

Dr. Rawlings accepted Christ at an early age and joined the Macedonia Baptist Church (MBC) in Arlington, Virginia. Dr. Rawlings quickly became an active disciple at MBC by ministering music through her gift of singing. Since then Dr. Rawlings has served as directress of MBC's Mass and Youth Choirs; leader of the Praise and Worship Team; Minister of Generation Now, Youth and Young Adult Ministry, and most recently as the associate pastor of administration.

Although Dr. Rawlings initially ministered through her gift of singing, in January 2006 she answered God's call to preach the Gospel. Two years later, in July 2008, she was officially licensed to preach. With license in hand, Dr. Rawlings was equipped and ready to do more to win souls for Jesus Christ. In June 2012, Dr. Rawlings was one of seven ministers chosen to preach for the Hampton University Ministers Conference first-ever series, New Emerging Voices.

As God has given Dr. Rawlings a passion for His people, He has also placed in her heart the desire to see young ladies and women become all God has designed them to be. In October 2010, Dr. Rawlings founded Jireh's Place, an organization dedicated to young ladies and young mothers in need of an adequate support system to help diffuse the daily educational, economic, and social challenges that all too often determine the destiny of our young people. In January 2013, Dr. Rawlings launched The Fellowship, a ministry for women that empowers, equips, and transforms the lives of women everywhere by meeting them where they are and channeling them to where they are purposed to be in Christ.

Dr. Rawlings is supported by her loving husband, Dawud Rawlings. They are the proud parents of Amena Rawlings. (Source: Dr. Shakina Dunbar Rawlings)

Ernest E. Johnson (Recreation Leader)

In 1949 Arlington established a formal Department of Recreation for the rapidly growing and developing county. However, the classes, clubs, and activities sponsored by the Department mirrored the school system and were segregated. In 1950 a formal Negro Recreation Section was created "with a special emphasis on sports." Its director was Ernest E. Johnson, who was a central figure for African Americans in Arlington who wished to participate in the Department's programs.

Johnson expanded the Negro Recreation Section to include classes for children, not only in a variety of sports, but dance, theater, music (including accordion classes), and community events like teen beauty pageants and parades, as well. He was forward-thinking, documenting many of these activities in the early- to mid-1950s with professional photographs; a collection of seventy-eight images are held in the community archives. Johnson oversaw the development of the Jennie Dean field and a new recreation center at Hoffman-Boston on South Queen Street. This center later became known as the Carver Center. Johnson's activities stretched beyond the Department of Recreation. He was the leader of Arlington's first African American Cub Scout Pack (#589), chartered in April of 1952.

For the 1962-1963 fiscal years, the Negro Recreation Section was quietly changed to the Carver Section, with Johnson still as its supervisor. In 1964 the Negro Recreation Section disappeared in a departmental reorganization; Johnson became supervisor of the Centers Section, overseeing "teen clubs, free classes, and meetings of non-Department sponsored clubs in the centers." With no fanfare at all, the County's Department of Recreation had become desegregated, and Johnson was integrated into the department's existing administration.

Ernest Johnson continued to serve Arlington County and, on May 8, 1982, Arlington celebrated Ernest E. Johnson Day with a parade that ran from the Walter Reed Recreation Center to the Carver Recreation Center, a softball game that afternoon, a senior tea, and a testimonial dinner that evening. Mrs. Mignon Johnson, wife of Ernest, taught at the Drew Elementary School. Johnson died in December 1992, after a life of service to the people of Arlington. His work let Arlington play. (Source: Excerpted from the Internet)

Solomon H. Thompson (1887-1983)

Mr. Solomon H. Thompson was born near Ft. Myer, Virginia. As one of the pioneer's in the development of this community, he believed first in the establishment of the three, fundamental institutions; namely home, school, and church. He labored arduously for all three. He also believed that a respected and progressive community was a voting community.

Alice Strother

Mrs. Alice Strother, one of the first crossing guards to be assigned in Arlington County, was charged with the duty of caring for the safety of our children as they proceeded to and from school. The fact that she performed her duty well is evidenced by her being selected for the Outstanding Citizenship Award by the Civitan Club in 1956.

Reverend Henry H. Sink

Reverend Henry H. Sink and his wife, Mrs. Mayme W. Sink, came to Lomax the first Sunday in October 1955 from Johnson City, Tennessee. He had nearly twenty-five years of preaching and pastoral experience. His accumulated knowledge of church administration and personal counseling during these years fitted him for the task of helpful service in any community where he was called.

Reverend Sink served efficiently and satisfactorily as a minister of the Gospel, a man called of God and dedicated to his work in the following Stations in Zion: St. Peter in Cleveland, Ohio; St. Mark in Indianapolis, Indiana; Hood Temple in Evansville, Indiana; Stoner Memorial in Louisville, Kentucky; Hauser Chapel in Pensacola, Florida; and St. Paul in Johnson City, Tennessee.

A graduate of the class of 1916 of Storer College in Harpers Ferry, West Virginia, he attended religious education classes at Western Reserve University in Cleveland, Ohio; Indiana University Extension in Indianapolis, Indiana; University of Evansville in Evansville, Indiana; and he majored in social science and psychology at Municipal College, a branch of the University of Louisville in Louisville, Kentucky.

He was an active member of the Arlington Ministerial Association; the Arlington Council of Churches; the Council of Churches of the National Church Area; the A.M.E. Zion Minister's Alliance; the Methodist Ministers Union of Washington and Vicinity; the International Ministers Union of Washington and Vicinity; the Board of Management of Veterans Memorial YMCA; and the Nauck Citizens Association.

Reverend Sherman W. Phillips

Reverend Sherman W. Phillips was born in Falls Church, Virginia. He confessed religion in 1912 at the First Baptist Church in Merrifield. He received his theological training at the Samuel Miller's School, Frelinghsen University in Washington, D.C. He was ordained in 1921. He was called to the Macedonia Baptist Church in August of 1925 and served as its pastor for forty-plus years. He was an inspiration to all and an asset to the Nauck community. (Source of above articles: the Internet)

Edward D. Strother

Mr. Edward D. Strother was born in The Plains, Virginia, and was married to Alice C. Strother. The Strother's had one daughter, Edna H., and have been residents of Arlington County since 1938. In Arlington County, Mr. Strother displayed an outstanding interest in civic matters and in our schools. His work in the procurement of the first addition to Drew School and in the efforts to obtain suitable facilities at Hoffman-Boston High School is well-known. The highest of esteem with which we hold him in the community him is evidenced by the various offices which he has held among which may be included past president of Drew-Kemper PTA, president of Hoffman-Boston PTA, president of Nauck Citizens Association, and member of the Executive Committee of A.B.C.

Mr. Strother was also a deacon of St. John's Baptist Church, a member of Citizens Committee of School Improvements, a member of Unitarians Layman's League, and a member of the Citizens Committee for Social Progress. He was the Political Action Chairman for NAACP, Arlington Branch. (Source: Internet article)

Anna P. Belcher

Mrs. Anna P. Belcher, wife of William W. Belcher of Washington, D.C., was truly one of the outstanding women of our community. During their forty-two years of married life, she and her husband raised four children: Mrs. Clare B. Simms; Mr. William W. Belcher, Jr.; Mrs. Edith B. Tate; and Mr. Harold P. Belcher.

Her work in the various civic organizations, both local and national, was well-known. The residents in the Nauck area liked to point with pride to her work in the organization of the Veterans Memorial Branch of the YMCA because she served as the moving spirit for this project. During the time in which she served as chairman of the Building Fund Committee, more than $20,000 was raised. Among many other things, she served on the first jury that admitted woman jurors. She also served three years on the Executive Committee. She was crowned first "Quota Queen" by actress Peggy Wood, in the 1954 drive of the Residential Unit of the Chest Federation, Metropolitan area. She was a life member of the National Council of Negro Women and served on the NCNW Youth Consenuation Committee (subcommittee of the White House Conference for Children and Youth). She was Arlington Delegate to the Convention of National Foundation for Infantile Paralysis at Tuskegee Institute in Alabama from 1949 to 1950.

Further she served as a member of the Arlington Interracial Commission for several years; was delegated by the County Board to name Jennie Dean Playground; was delegated by the Federal Government to name a major housing project, the George Washington Carver Homes, for which she worked arduously for several years; and was named "Woman of the Year" in 1953 by the Virginia State Federation of Colored Women's Clubs. A clerk for eighteen years in the U.S. Department of Labor, she received the Meritorious Service Award in 1945 and an Efficiency Award for a useful suggestion in 1948. (Source: Internet article)

Jenny Davis

A new housing complex in Arlington is to be named for Jennie Davis (Family Photo)

Jennie T. Davis was raised in Baltimore, Maryland, and moved to Arlington with her husband, James Davis, in 1976. While exploring the housing market in Arlington, the Davis' were denied the opportunity to view certain homes because of the color of their skin. As a result of her experience, Jennie not only realized individuals had limited housing possibilities due to discrimination, but there was also a lack of affordable housing in the community. This ignited a flame within her to pursue social justice and equality in Arlington. Through her work to expose discriminatory housing practices and emphasize the need and importance of affordable housing, Jennie Davis co-founded AHC, Inc., an organization heavily involved in providing quality, affording housing and programs to assist families in building strong futures. Mrs. Davis was instrumental in the creation of AHC's Home Improvement Program (HIP) and the Moderate Income Home Ownership

Program (MIHOP). As a community leader, Jennie Davis served as president of the Nauck Civic Association for more than twenty years; member of the Community Development Citizens' Advisory Committee for several years; and on the AHC board as the longest-serving member. (Source: Internet Article)

John Robinson, Jr.

John Robinson, Jr. was born in Arlington County in 1934 to the late John Robinson, Sr. and Faith A. Robinson. John attended the Arlington County Public Schools and attended Kemper Elementary and Hoffman-Boston High School at a time when Arlington public education institutions were segregated. He later attended Howard University in Washington, D.C. and served in the U.S. Army for six months.

John helped to break down the segregation barriers during the late 1950s and early 1960s in Northern Virginia, in areas such as housing, food counters, movie theatres, etc. He picketed and protested and stood firm in his convictions and beliefs. John always believed African Americans should have equal rights at a time when they did not. He worked diligently to register new voters in the African American communities of Arlington and Northern Virginia. John also conducted numerous surveys and tallies to compile statistics and other information to assess the needs of the minorities in the community.

John worked closely with politicians, the criminal justice system, and the Arlington County Police Department to get drugs and drug pushers off the streets so that children, families, and senior citizens could feel safe. John also coordinated food, clothing, and furniture drives for many needy families, and he has opened his doors to hundreds of homeless in the area. He diligently sought ways to better working relationships between the African American and Hispanic communities in Arlington.

John worked as a committed and dedicated community activist in Arlington for over thirty years. In 1965 he began employment with the U.P.O. office at 2411South Kenmore Street, and the name of the center was changed to the Arlington Community Action Committee and later to the Arlington Community Action Program. In the late 1970s, the name of the center was changed to the Martin Luther King, Jr. Community Center, in honor of the late Reverend Dr. Martin Luther King, Jr. John was on call there, twenty-four hours per day, seven days per week.

Over the years, Robinson was active in organizations, including: the Veterans Memorial YMCA; Congress of Racial Equality (C.O.R.E.); the Nauck Civic Association; Action Coordinating Committee to End Segregation in the Suburbs (ACCESS); Southern Christian Leadership Conference; and the United Planning Organization. He was instrumental in the planning of the Arlington County Action Program in the 1960s.

In the early 1960s, he became the publisher of the community newsletter, the *Green Valley News*, a free publication that circulated for more than four decades. (Source: Internet Article)

Thaddenia Hayes West

In the early 1940s, a group of devout and determined African American Catholics, including Mrs. Thaddenia West, Joseph Bowman, Clarence and Selens Brown, Alice Butler, Lawrence and Jessie Butler, Irma Carter, Hattie Ellis, Mary Fernanders, Edward Marshall, Grace McGwinn, Edward and Alice Moorman, Constance Spencer, and Sophia Terry, met in the home of Edward and Alice Moorman to make plans to build a Catholic church where they could worship in dignity. By 1945 they were able to obtain a meeting with a representative of the Richmond Diocese, then responsible for Arlington County, to discuss establishing a parish for African American Catholics. The group became the founders of Our Lady Queen of Peace. (Source: Internet Article)

Mrs. West died in 2012. She is survived by her devoted children: Raquel Hall, Beverly Goode and Clifton N. West (Carol); her nine grandchildren; her sixteen great-grandchildren; and her three great-great-grandchildren, as well as many loving relatives and friends.

Portia A. Clark

When Portia Clark was born in 1959, Nauck had two African American doctors: Dr. Bruner and Dr. Butler. Her mother was a patient of Dr. Butler. One year before Portia was born, her mother went to see him on a Friday when she was not feeling good. He gave her a doctor's slip for admission to Freedmen's Hospital in D.C. He told her she was pregnant and was not going to make it through the weekend. Sure enough, she delivered Portia's brother who, people used to say, was the tumor she thought she had. She continued to see Dr. Butler when Portia was born. It was a few years after Portia's birth when Arlington Hospital would allow African American births. During those days, the African American community was built to meet their needs. People had a doctor, nurse, beautician, barber, and an insurance man who could make home visits and take care of families.

Mrs. Clark remembers her first teacher at Drew, Mrs. Bea Richardson. The Clarks lived around the corner from Drew on South Lowell Street in what is now called Ft. Henry Gardens. Mrs. Clark enjoyed going to school and would run from home to get to class early. She was in the old wing. That wing became the community center before the building was demolished. She attended Drew before desegregation with all African American students and teachers who cared about the children and the community. Her mother was not active in school activities like some parents were, but she sent her children to school to get an education, which she was not so privileged to have. She went to school up to the eighth grade before dropping out to work and help take care of her family.

The three most memorable teachers Mrs. Clark had at Drew where she went until the sixth grade were Mrs. Richardson, Mrs. Hazeltine Harris, and Mr. Hardy Williams. She was in Mrs. Harris' class for the fourth and fifth grades. It was in her class where the students all cried when they heard the news that Dr. Martin Luther King, Jr. was assassinated. The children could all relate to the times and were taught to understand what it meant. Dr. King was a great leader who made a difference, even today with his dream. Mrs. Clark remembers Ms. Harris for her kindness and generosity. Twice she allowed Mrs. Clark and her girlfriends to go home with her for the weekend to spend the night. She lived in Washington, D.C. at the time and was married to a D.C. policeman. Today Mrs. Harris is a well-known teacher by many. Before and after her retirement, she did Title I and was a storyteller. This is how Mrs. Clark's children got to know her for her stories. They will never forget "Did You Feed My Cow?" The third most memorable teacher was Mr. Hardy Williams, her sixth grade teacher. Mrs. Clark became a real entrepreneur and put her math skills to work running a candy store from her locker. Her mother ran the food counter at the Green Valley Pharmacy. Mrs. Clark went to work with her before school started and would open the candy store for Dr. Muse and ring up sales until she went to school. The store became the supplier for her candy store. Mrs. Clark would sell mostly Now-N-Laters, Mary Jane's, Squirrel Nuts, and bubble gum. Mr. Williams was remembered for teaching her math and discipline. The first day of classes, he introduced the students to his leather belt that was wrapped with masking tape. He never used it on the girls, but if the boys mis-behaved, he would bring them to the front of the room and use his belt in front of the class. Many of the students grew up that sixth grade year. They tried a lot, and they learned a lot. Mrs. Clark even got suspended from school by the prin-cipal, Mr. Cooley, for watching a fight after school. On January fifteenth every year after the assassination of Dr. Martin Luther King, Jr., the students would skip school. That year Mrs. Clark thinks the whole class went to the Mall in D.C. for the protest. She believes it was the year Stevie Wonder rewrote the Birthday song. School was never the same after leaving Drew. The children were bused out of the neighborhood. Most of the students in Nauck were split between Gunston and Hoffman-Boston.

Mrs. Clark started junior high school at Gunston. Her mom and dad split, and they moved. She ended up at Thomas Jefferson Annex, which was at Hoffman-Boston. The next year, she was in the first class to attend T.J., the school without walls. She left T.J. and returned to Hoffman-Boston, which became a new model program that is now at HB-Woodlawn, a school with opportunities for students to work independently. The students called teachers by their first name and de-veloped their own schedules. Teachers were like hippies or those who grew up in the '60s with the civil rights movement and flower power. There was little or no structure. The students made up their own field trips.

Portia Clark is known as a community activist who has worked in the Arlington community for over thirty years. Her activism began when her children grew up, starting with the Arlington Public Schools. Next she became actively engaged with the Nauck Civic Association and that led to the Community Association of Resources for Education, Enrichment & Economics (CARE), Inc., the non-profit organization that she founded in 1996.

She is currently in a transition stage, planning her retirement after thirty-four years of government service. She con-tinues to serve those in need with a focus on disadvantaged communities. Her professional development and training has afforded her the titles of Information Management Officer, Diversity Program Manager, Executive Planning Officer, and Project Manager. Her career has been blended with assignments in human resources and information technology. Today she manages and provides accommodations for people with disabilities. Her community focus blends the work she does with youth and seniors into a concierge of support and services that are needed. Her vision today is to create sustainable communities that will allow others to age in place with the support and the services needed to remain safe and comfortable at home and actively engaged in life and living.

Working with the Arlington Villages Project is helping her to further develop her vision and her passion for helping others. Her community, Nauck, is a model community to pilot a program for a diverse population of elderly residents aging in place. She will continue to maintain a residence in Arlington, where she has lived all her life. As the primary operator of PC Homes, LLC, a company that is developing affordable housing for young adults and elderly, she provides needed support and services. (Information furnished by Mrs. Portia Clark)

Vivian S. Bullock

Vivian Bullock was born in Arlington, Virginia, on April 21, 1923. She was educated in the Public School Systems of Arlington, Virginia, and Washington, D.C., where she was always interested in learning. After high school, she continued numerous, higher courses of interest. In 1947 she married Granderson Bullock of Nauck, and they have one daughter, Jacqueline Limas.

Vivian retired from the Federal Government after thirty years of service, where the highlights of her experiences include work on several presidential committees required to report on civil rights. She was also active in her community as a member of Lomax A.M.E. Zion and Calloway United Methodist Churches. She served as a member of community and charitable organizations, which included the Board of Directors of the Veterans Memorial YMCA and a charter member of the Y's Menettes, the National Council of Negro Women, the Nauck Civic Association, and the Black History Committee.

When massive resistance became Virginia's policy to prevent desegregation in the wake of *Brown v. Board of Education* in 1954, Prince Edward County refused to integrate its schools and closed its entire public school system. There were many African American students who wanted to continue their education. Two students from Farmville, Virginia, came to Arlington for schooling, and one became a part of Vivian and Granderson's family. Both attended and graduated from Hoffman-Boston High School.

The Congress of Equal Equality (CORE) sponsored a project that resulted in picketing at the Arlington and Buckingham theatres. It was the beginning of a summer of protest in which several members (of which Vivian was one) were arrested and charged to provide the impetus for a test case. The American Civil Liberties Union (ACKU) lawyers argued the case and all were acquitted.

She is actively pursuing many of her favorite hobbies in her senior years. She loves line dancing with family members and seniors at the Thomas Jefferson Community Center, oil painting at the Walter Reed Center, and still enjoys a good bridge game. (Source: Vivian Bullock)

Pauline Johnson Ferguson

Pauline Johnson Ferguson, the youngest child of Bonder and Amanda Johnson (founders of the Macedonia Baptist Church), was born on October 31, 1906, in Washington, D.C. She was one of fifteen children born to this union. She was baptized in 1917 by Reverend Randolph at Mt. Moriah Baptist Church, in Washington, D.C. and, later in that year, joined the Macedonia Baptist Church.

Not only was Mrs. Ferguson active in her church, but was also active in her community. She held various positions in the church. For forty years, she served as the church clerk and was president of the Never Idle Club for thirty-four years. She was a member of the October Calendar Club and the Deaconess Board, on which she served for forty-three years.

She was just as dedicated to the Nauck community and served as a charter member of the Y's Menettes Service Club of the Veterans Memorial YMCA, where she also served on the Board of Management. She took great pride in being recognized as one of the top recruiters for the Arlington Branch NAACP in its Annual Membership Drive, as well as her membership in the Nauck Civic Association. Whatever the activity or cause, you could always count on her to be a "drum major" and help lead it.

She was employed at the White House during the Harry S. Truman, Dwight D. Eisenhower, John F. Kennedy, Lyndon Baines Johnson, and Richard M. Nixon administrations in the housekeeping department and counted among her great memories that each summer she travelled to Hyannis Point, Massachusetts, to open the summer home of President John F. Kennedy. She retired during President Richard M. Nixon's first term in office. Her husband, Carl W. Ferguson, was also employed at the White House, where he served as a doorman for eleven years and the World Bank, where he retired after seventeen years.

On July 29, 1983, Mrs. Ferguson was voted Mother of the Church, a title she proudly cherished until her passing in December of 1990. (Source: Family oral history)

Robert (Bob) Winkler

Robert Winkler was born in Washington, D.C. on June 5, 1942. He moved to Arlington, Virginia, from Bailey's Crossroads, where he attended James Lee Elementary School. He continued his education at the Hoffman Boston Junior and Senior High Schools and the Northern Virginia Community College. After schooling he entered the United States Army, in which he served four years of active duty. Upon his return in 1968, he married his next door neighbor, Juanita Simmons. At the time of his passing, they had enjoyed over forty years of marriage. Of this union, they had one son, Sidney, and four granddaughters, Makenzie Brooks-Winkler, Sydney Winkler, Taylor Winkler, and Brianna Paynes.

Bob loved the Nauck community. Whatever went on, he felt that he had to be a part of it, and he was. He was employed by the Department of Parks and Recreation for over forty years. He coached the Nauck youth and, in doing so, he made sure each kid who wanted to play could. He would pay their fee, pick them up, and take them home. Two of the young men who he made sure would play AA and travel as far as California were Kevin Gaskins and Joe Lowe. He made sure that children who could not otherwise were able to attend the Drew Recreation after school program. He knew parents had to work and some could not afford it, but he always make a way to enable their kids to attend. He would go to food banks or others to get snack foods for the children enrolled in the program and for the older children who attended the evening program.

Bob was an active member of the Nauck Civic Association and always made sure he was a part of all their activities. He played an active part in their efforts to have Drew designated as its community school so that its residents could go to the school in the community and not be bused out. He was also a charter member of the Y's Men's Organization, a service organization that supported the Veterans Memorial YMCA.

Bob was a wise man. Whatever he did, he would keep to himself. He never sought praise, and he felt good about what he had done within. To know Robert (Bob) Winkler was to love him because he had so much to give. He would let different singing groups rehearse in the center at no cost. He would work events with no pay so that families of Nauck could use it. (Contributed by wife, Juanita Winkler)

Joan E. Cooper

Joan E. Cooper, born on October 25, 1941, in Freedmen's Hospital, Washington, D.C., was the epitome of community service.

Growing up experiencing segregation in housing, education, and employment, she was determined to make a difference for herself and the community she loved. Joan began her career in community service, starting in the early '50s when she was involved in the Civil Rights Movement by being part of the Congress of Racial Equality and the Action Coordinating Committee to End Segregation in the Suburbs and when she volunteered with the Southern Christian Leadership Conference, even marching with Dr. Martin Luther King, Jr. in Mississippi.

Seeing a need in her own neighborhood, Joan founded the Parent Family Support Group, which created Arlington County's first drug patrol, Crack Down on Drug Patrol. With the help of the Arlington County Police Department, this program was a success in curbing the drug trafficking. As a result, the community had the pleasure of hosting former President George H.W. Bush. Most of Joan's career was spent with the Arlington Police Department, where she served as the only community service technician, further developing and serving the community and the Police Department.

Joan has served on or chaired nearly three dozen community service organizations. She is an active member of her church, Lomax AME Zion, as well as the Dorie Miller Unit 194 Auxiliary of the American Legion, the United Way, the

American Red Cross, and the Nauck Revitalization Organization. Although retired for several years, she is still committed to serving by recently completing a course at the Alexandria Department's Citizen's Police Academy in May 2013.

Joan is the daughter of the late Lloyd and Hattie Cooper. She is the mother of the late Carlton Cooper, and grandmother of Brandon Dunbar and Carlton Dunbar. She has six, great-grandchildren. She is the sister of Lloyd (Buddy) Cooper (Martina), the late Kenneth Cooper, (Pat), Iris Cooper McElroy, Dorise Cooper Kenney (Vernon), and Doris Cooper. She was a single parent but always wanted to wear that cap and gown and get a degree. She received her G.E.D. from Arlington County Adult Education and enrolled in Northern Virginia Community College, where she made the Dean's List. Her major was an Associate of Science Degree in General Studies. She is also taking Spanish and writing a book. (Submitted by Joan E. Cooper)

Laverne Roberts Langhorne

Laverne Roberts is a lifelong resident of the Nauck community. Her parents, Vernon and Elnora Roberts, lived in Arlington, Virginia, and in the early 1950s, many of the African American children living in Arlington (herself included) were born in Freedmen's Hospital in Washington, D.C.

She attended public schools in Arlington, which included: Kemper Elementary; Drew Elementary; Drew Annex; Hoffman-Boston; Thomas Jefferson Middle (Jr. High); and Wakefield High. Her daughter, Kimberly Roberts, also attended public schools in Arlington, and she graduated from Norfolk State University; she now lives back in Nauck.

Her parents were members of the Macedonia Baptist Church in Arlington, Virginia, and her brother, Vernon Roberts, Jr., and she also joined Macedonia. They were active members of the Sunday school, and she was a Sunday school teacher and former superintendent. Macedonia has always been a blessing for her, especially now that her parents have passed away. Most of the churches in Nauck have been the "backbone" of the community.

She is a member of Arlington County's NAACP and also the Nauck Civic Association, where she served as block captain and former recording secretary.

Sixty years ago, the residents in Nauck knew all of their neighbors, and now Nauck is quickly becoming a diverse community, affording the residents the chance to share their customs and lifestyles. Nauck has always been a great community to live. (Source: LaVerne Roberts)

Kimberly M. Roberts

Kimberly M. Roberts is a lifelong resident of Arlington, Virginia. She is the daughter of LaVerne Langhorn and Thomas Jones and older sister of Crystal Tucker. Both of her parents are also native Arlingtonians; specifically, the Nauck community. Kim attended Washington-Lee High School, graduating in 1988, and is a proud alumnus of Norfolk State University (NSU), class of 1993. She is an active member of the NSU Washington, D.C. Alumni Association.

Starting at an early age, Kim attended Macedonia Baptist Church and was active in Sunday school, where her mother was a teacher and Sunday school superintendent for over twenty years. Kim also served on the Junior Usher Board. As an adult, Kim rededicated her life to Jesus Christ and joined Shiloh Baptist Church in Lorton, Virginia, where she is active in the women's and newsletter ministries.

For over thirteen years, Kim has been employed by Advanced Systems Development Inc. (ASD) as a senior human resources generalist. In 2012 she received her certification as a Human Resources Professional from the Society of Human Resources Management. Her career began with Arlington Public Schools Transportation Department as a routing specialist.

As an active member in the Arlington County community, Kim is very involved in several different community organizations. She serves as the recording secretary of the Nauck Civic Association and is a member of the Black Heritage Museum of Arlington's Executive Board. She also volunteers her time with her affiliated political party.

Kim recently launched QT Gift Bags, a direct sell business that allows her to celebrate, encourage, and reward women.

Kim is an avid football fan, with the Pittsburgh Steelers as her favorite team. Her spare time is spent enjoying her family, friends, and "fur baby," Jayna. (Source: Kimberly Roberts)

Yolanda Johnson Black

One of Thomas H. West's granddaughters, Yolanda Johnson Black, is still active in the community. She is a lifelong member of the church he helped build, Lomax AME Zion. Starting as a young child in Buds of Promise, Tom Thumb weddings, and the youth choir to her current involvement as a member of the Life Member's Council, Lay Council, and Senior Ministry, she continues to be involved in church activities. She also served on the Lomax Community Development Corporation (Lomax Manor Housing Development) Board under the leadership of Reverend Cameron Jackson. As a member of this committee, she supported efforts to develop housing for the elderly on property owned by Lomax Church.

As a volunteer appointed by the Arlington County Board, she served on the Neighborhood Partnership Grants Committee, which is operated by the Arlington Community Foundation. In this role she reviewed for approval, applications for funds for community projects. She was also an active member of the Nauck Civic Association. In this organization, she forged a relationship with Jennie Davis, and through this association, she began supporting political fundraising projects, as well as housing development projects. Fundraising events she helped organize supported Douglas Wilder and other democrats involved in Virginia affairs. Her interest in affordable housing led her to become the president of the board of directors of the Arlington Housing Corporation (later to become AHC). This non-profit organization develops, sells, and/or offers for rent affordable housing, initially in Arlington, but now in the Mid- and South-Atlantic areas. While serving as president of the AHC Board, AHC renovated Westover Apartments (153 units), purchased a portion of and renovated Lee Gardens (Woodbury Park, 364 units), and purchased Arlington View (77 units). She served on AHC's Home Improvement Program, a program that grants funds to low-income residents to make repairs on their home. In the area of affordable housing, she was on the board of Westover Apartments, an AHC-owned complex in Arlington that offers affordable housing. Currently she serves on the AHC advisory Committee, where she reviews developed properties, including the activities of AHCs of the for-profit AHC Management Company. She is also a founding member of Borremeo Housing, a program that offers two group homes and other support for single mothers.

Professionally she was the first civilian African American manager of an officer's club at Ft Belvoir. Later she became the general manager of a hotel in Washington, D.C., which housed the leaders of the Civil Rights Movement, including Martin Luther King, Jesse Jackson, Andrew Young, Ralph Abernathty, and Congressman Lewis. She provided assistance to them in arranging facilities for meetings, arranging food, babysitting for their children, and transportation to protests and activities, including "Resurrection City" and the 1965 March on Washington. (Source: Yolanda Johnson Black)

Esther Georgia Irving Cooper

Esther Cooper was born on November 28, 1881, in Cleveland, Ohio, and was the daughter of William Irving and Katherine Harris Irving. Her mother's family, who had secured their freedom before the Civil War, arrived in Ohio from North Carolina in the 1850s. Nothing is known of Esther Irving's education. She began working for Harry Clay Smith, the first African American member of the Ohio legislature and editor of the *Cleveland Gazette*. Early in the 1910s, in Louisville, Kentucky, she assisted Nannie Helen Burroughs, then corresponding secretary of the Woman's Convention Auxiliary of the National Baptist Convention, in raising funds for Burroughs's recently opened National Training School for Women and Girls (later the National Trade and Professional School for Women and Girls), located in Washington, D.C.

After moving to Washington in 1913 to work as a stenographer in the Forest Service of the U.S. Department of Agriculture, Irving met George Posea Cooper, a Tennessee native and veteran of the Philippine Insurrection, then serving as a technical sergeant in the Quartermaster Corps at Fort Myer in Alexandria County (after 1920 Arlington County). They married on September 10, 1913, and had three daughters. The family highly valued books and education and, according to one daughter, acquired an encyclopedia set before they had electricity or indoor plumbing. Cooper resigned from government service in the mid-1920s, but she continued part-time work teaching classes in English, shorthand, and typing at the National Training School for Women and Girls. In 1934 and 1935, she conducted business classes in the adult education program of the Arlington County Public Schools as part of the Federal Education Rehabilitation Act. After her husband died on October 23, 1937, she sought unsuccessfully to regain full-time, government employment.

Cooper devoted much of her time to improving educational opportunities for African American children. Dissatisfied with the inferior facilities and textbooks offered in the African American schools in Arlington County, she sent her own daughters to Washington, D.C., for their secondary education. They lived with an uncle during the week and returned home to Arlington for weekends. Cooper joined the Kemper School Parent-Teacher Association and served as its president for several years. As secretary of the education committee of the Hoffman-Boston School in 1935, she began lobbying Arlington school officials to establish an accredited junior high school in the County. In 1940 Cooper organized and became first president of the Arlington County branch of the National Association for the Advancement of Colored People. Two years later, she joined the executive board of the Virginia State Conference of the NAACP. In collaboration with State NAACP leaders and lawyers, the Arlington branch initiated a court case, challenging inequalities in the County's high school facilities. Their efforts culminated in *Carter v. School Board of Arlington County* (1950), in which the Fourth Circuit Court of Appeals ruled that the County's separate high schools constituted unlawful racial discrimination.

As NAACP branch president during the 1940s, Cooper linked her local community to the broader statewide and national efforts to achieve voting rights and equal treatment for African Americans. She supported initiatives to abolish the poll tax and wrote letters to Arlington officials protesting segregation on public transportation and in public facilities. A member of the Southern Conference for Human Welfare, an interracial organization founded in 1938 that focused on social and economic problems in the South, Cooper served as president of the SCHW's Arlington chapter and chaired the Eighth District Committee for Virginia. She also supported the activities of the Southern Negro Youth Congress, a civil rights group advocating improvements in education, employment, and health care for African Americans. Among the organizers of the SNYC in Richmond in 1937 were her daughter, Esther Victoria Cooper, an editor of *Freedomways* from 1961 to 1985, and her future son-in-law, James Edward Jackson, later a prominent Communist Party activist. In 1947 Cooper ran for a seat on Arlington County's Democratic Executive Committee, but she was one of six progressive candidates disqualified from appearing on the primary ballot for allegedly failing to comply with party regulations. She retired as president of the county NAACP branch in 1951 but remained active as its president emerita.

Cooper participated in numerous community improvement organizations. She joined Saint John's Baptist Church in 1914 and served as president of the Baptist Young People's Union. A charter member of Arlington County's chapter of the Virginia Council of Church Women, she was, for many years, a vice president of the Lott Carey Foreign Mission Society. During the mid-1940s, she lobbied on behalf of the Citizens Committee for School Improvement. Cooper helped organize the Jennie Dean Community Center Association, a women's group that raised money to purchase land for a recreation center open to African Americans. The association acquired several lots, and in 1947, she donated them to the Veterans Memorial Branch of the Young Men's Christian Association. As secretary of the Butler Holmes Citizens Association, Cooper registered voters and sought to end the poll tax as a prerequisite for voting. She continued working on political campaigns and at polling places through the 1964 presidential election.

Cooper suffered cardiac arrest and died at her Arlington County home on February 7, 1970. She was buried next to her husband's grave in Arlington National Cemetery. (Contributed by Larissa M. Smith and the *Dictionary of Virginia Biography*)

Law and Politics

Judge Thomas R. Monroe
Bobby B. Stafford, Esq.
Charles P. Monroe, Esq.
Luttrelle F. Parker, Esq.
Robert M. Alexander, Esq.

Judge Thomas R. Monroe

Thomas Monroe Dies at 80; Arlington Judge
Thomas R. Monroe was a community activist for years before his appointment as a judge.
By Patricia Sullivan, *Washington Post* Staff Writer
Sunday, January 30, 2005; Page C11

Thomas Randolph Monroe, eighty, the first African American judge in Arlington County, as well as the first judge to serve on all three Arlington courts, died of congestive heart failure on January 28, 2005, at Virginia Hospital Center in Arlington.

Judge Monroe served on the bench from 1972 until illness forced his retirement in 1993. When he retired, then Chief Circuit Judge William L. Winston said his legacy was his compassion as well as his competence.

He was tough when circumstances called for it, but above all, he was compassionate. "I never saw him do a mean thing," Winston said at the time.

An Arlington County Bar Association award named after Winston was presented to Judge Monroe in 2000. He was the first African American member of that bar association.

Born in the Eastern Shore's Northampton County, near Cape Charles, Virginia, Judge Monroe worked as a caddy at a whites-only golf course and was a star center fielder for the town's baseball team. He graduated from Johnson C. Smith University in Charlotte and served as a sergeant in the Army in the Pacific and European theaters during World War II. He received his law degree from Howard University in 1951 and set up a private law practice in Arlington the next year.

He practiced law for twenty years and quickly established himself as a civic leader, serving as president of the Arlington chapter of the NAACP in 1955 and circulating a petition to desegregate Arlington's schools. Into the early 1970s, he stayed in the struggle, joining a group of parents whose children attended the all-African American Drew Elementary School in a desegregation suit against the county.

He became a substitute judge in Juvenile and Domestic Relations Court in 1972, a General District Court judge in 1976, and the state's second African American Circuit Court judge in 1982.

Judge Monroe was on the board of directors of the Arlington County Action Program. He was president of the Nauck Citizens Association and on the county's criminal justice advisory committee and its human relations commission. He was a member of the Kappa Alpha Psi Fraternity and an avid golfer.

One of his sons, Charles P. Monroe, an Arlington County Board member, died in 2003 during his first regular meeting as chairman.

Survivors include his wife of forty-nine years, Eleanor Ames Monroe, who was the first African American member of the Arlington School Board; a son, Thomas R. Monroe Jr., of Fairfax County; a daughter, Patricia M. Meek of Fairfax

County; a sister, Beatrice Ames of Arlington; a brother, James Monroe of Cranberry, New Jersey; and six grandchildren. (Source: Internet article)

Bobby B. Stafford, Esq.

"If any feather is to be placed in his cap, he would be satisfied with accolades for his help and involvement in developing leaders and launching the careers of young people in the field of law."

Bobby B. Stafford, Esq., credits his early childhood spent on his aunt and uncle's farm in Williamsburg County, South Carolina, with instilling in him sensitivity toward others, a generous spirit, and a sense of kindness and fairness that would foster his passion for social justice. That nurturing environment planted the seeds for a successful legal career and outstanding community service.

He received his undergraduate degree at North Carolina A&T State University in Greensboro and earned his law degree at Howard University, where he met his wife, Attorney Mary Raby. After passing the bar in South Carolina, they returned to Washington, D.C. to begin a storied legal career that would span more than thirty-five years. Stafford joined the law firm of his father-in-law, James H. Raby of Alexandria, Virginia, which later became the Firm of Raby and Stafford. Stafford's litigation of cases in Virginia and the District of Columbia, where he is a member of the courts of the District and local and federal courts of Northern Virginia, helped to establish his reputation as an attorney who would accept difficult and challenging cases involving real property, general civil and civil rights law, and criminal trial work. The Firm is known for its willingness to accept cases unappealing to other law firms because of their focus on social justice issues.

As passionate as he is about the legal field, Attorney Stafford's record in community service is equally noteworthy. He has served for eight years on the Board of Visitors and as a founding member of the Athletic Foundation, Inc., of Norfolk State University in Virginia. He serves as president of the Arlington Community Action Program; general counsel and steward board member of the Campbell AME Church, advisory board of the Alexandria Urban League; general counsel of the Martin Luther King, Jr., Community Center, Inc.; and commissioner in Chancery for Arlington County. His other affiliations include the Arlington Hospital Board, National Bar Association, Washington Bar Association, Omega Psi Phi Fraternity, and the national committee on by-laws of the Sigma Pi Phi Fraternity of the Boule. He is a former appointed commissioner for selection of United States Magistrates for the United States District Court for the Eastern District of Virginia, where he served for approximately twenty years.

Stafford has also been active in politics, leading the campaign of former Congresswoman Shirley Chisholm's campaign for President in 1972, serving as a delegate to the 1972 Democratic National Convention, working with former President Jimmy Carter's campaign, and hosting events for former Virginia Lieutenant Governor and Governor Chuck Robb. Stafford received the Governor's appointment as Escheator for the City of Alexandria, which affords the opportunity to sell property on behalf of the state, and as a commissioner for Interpreting the Arts for the Executive Mansion of the Governor.

He and his wife are the parents of a daughter, Stacy L. Stafford, also an attorney. (Source: Internet article)

Charles P. Monroe (Former County Board Chairman)

Charles P. Monroe was a native Arlingtonian. He was elected to the County Board in 1999, served as Vice Chairman in 2002 and was elected as the 2003 Chairman at the Board's January 1, 2003, Organizational Meeting. He represented the County Board on the Metropolitan Washington Council of Governments' Human Services Policy Committee and Water Supply Task Force, as well as the Northern Virginia Regional Commission. He was also an alternate to the Metropolitan Washington Council of Governments' Chesapeake Bay Task Force.

Prior to taking office on January 1, 2000, Mr. Monroe was a civic activist, seeking minority participation in County government and politics. He was also an advocate for affordable housing and other issues affecting the financially disadvantaged. Mr. Monroe served in a variety of civic organizations and advisory groups, including: Arlington Human Rights Commission, 1990-95 (Chairman, 1992-95); Arlington Housing Corporation Board of Directors, 1994-1999 (President, 1997-98); Arlington Board of Zoning Appeals, 1995-99 (Vice Chairman, 1999); Veteran's Memorial Y.M.C.A. Committee of Management, 1997-2003; Arlington Chapter of the National Association for the Advancement of Colored People (NAACP.); and Arlington Kiwanis, 2000-2003.

Mr. Monroe was an attorney with the law firm of Duncan & Hopkins, P.C. in Old Town, Alexandria, where he was a civil litigator. He is survived by his wife Barbara, and their sons, Christopher and Jonathan, who live in the Glencarlyn neighborhood of south Arlington. His sons attend Arlington County Public Schools. He was a member of Mount Zion Baptist Church in Arlington, Virginia.

Mr. Monroe graduated from Yorktown High School. He obtained his Bachelor of Arts in political science at Duke University and his Juris Doctor degree from the Washington & Lee University School of Law. (Source: Internet article)

Luttrelle F. Parker, Esq.

The Honorable Lutrelle Fleming Parker Sr. was born in Newport News, Virginia, on March 10, 1924. He had been a long-term resident of Arlington County, Virginia, before his death on December 16, 1994.

Mr. Parker was a 1947 civil engineering graduate of Howard University. Prior to joining the United States Patent Office (the predecessor of the U.S. Patent and Trademark Office) in 1947, he had already served a combined five years in the government and military. When he joined the Patent Office, Mr. Parker was one of the rare African American patent examiners on the job. While employed at the Patent Office, he was one of the first four African Americans accepted at Georgetown Law School. He graduated from the Georgetown University Law School in 1952. He later worked as an attorney in the Office of the Solicitor of the Patent Office.

Mr. Parker served with particular distinction from 1961 through June, 1970, in the Solicitor's Office. He received a Superior Accomplishment Award in 1962 and the Commerce Department's second highest award, the Meritorious Service Award (Silver Medal), in 1963. In 1964 he was the recipient of a Department of Commerce Science and Technology Fellowship (later serving as president of the Fellows). Mr. Parker served on the Johnson Commission (called for by President Lyndon B. Johnson), which made recommendations on Patent Office reform. On June 10, 1970, Mr. Parker received a Presidential Certificate of Commendation from President Nixon for exceptional service to others. He was listed in *Who's Who in Government* in 1972.

Toward the end of his tenure in the Solicitor's Office, on March 11, 1970, Mr. Parker was nominated for a position as an Examiner-in-Chief on the Board of Patent Appeals by President Richard Nixon. He was confirmed by the Senate on May 14, 1970. He was sworn in by Secretary Maurice Stans on June 29, 1970, as the first African American to hold such a position.

Mr. Parker was nominated for the position of Deputy Commissioner of Patents and Trademarks on December 30, 1974, by President Gerald R. Ford. He was confirmed by the Senate on February 11, 1975, and sworn in on March 8, 1975. He was the first African American to hold that position.

He served as Acting Commissioner of Patents and Trademarks from August 1977 to June 1978, the first African American to hold the position of Commissioner in any capacity. Again, in 1979, Mr. Parker was appointed Acting Commissioner of Patents and Trademarks following the resignation of Donald Banner by President Jimmy Carter. He was the first African American to hold that position. He returned to his position on the Board of Patent Appeals in 1980, where he stayed through its reorganization as the Board of Patent Appeals and Interferences until he retired in 1986. In 1995 the U.S. Patent and Trademark Office named its law library after Mr. Parker. The Lutrelle F. Parker Sr. Memorial Law Library was dedicated on June 19, 1995, and is located in Crystal Park One, Room 568.

During his military career in the Navy, Mr. Parker served as a gunnery officer aboard an AKA in the Pacific Ocean during World War II. After leaving the active military, Mr. Parker was commissioned upon graduation from the U.S. Naval Reserve Midshipman's School at Cornell University, becoming one of the earliest African American Navy Officers. Mr. Parker rose to the Navy rank of Captain. Captain Parker completed Senior Naval Reserve Officers' Courses at the United States Naval War College, in Newport, Rhode Island. While in the Naval Reserve, Captain Parker was Commanding Officer of Reserve Crew U.S.S. Steinaker (DD-863); Commanding Officer of Reserve Crew U.S.S. Allen Sumner (DD-692); Commanding Officer of Military Training Division 5-1; and Commanding Officer of a shore patrol station in New York City. On July 9, 1974, Captain Parker (at the time, the highest ranking African American naval reserve officer in the Washington, D.C. Metropolitan area) took command of Destroyer Atlantic Detachment 406. He was the first African American commander of the Destroyer detachment. During this command, he supported the regular naval forces of Destroyer Squadron 30, which was comprised of six ships. He retired from the U.S. Navy Reserve in 1992.

As an Arlington County resident, Mr. Parker was active in civic activities. He was the first African American to serve as a member and, subsequently, Chairman of the Arlington County Planning Commission. He was a member of the Arlington County Zoning Appeals Board and President of the Nauck Citizens Association. He was a member of the Board of Management of the Veterans Memorial YMCA in Arlington. He was a member of the Board of Directors of the Arlington Metropolitan Chorus; a member of the Board of Visitors of George Mason University of Virginia (where he helped found the George Mason School of Law); and chairman of the Long Range Planning and Zoning Committee at George Mason University in Virginia. Mr. Parker was also Vice President of the Board of Trustees at Arlington Hospital; a member of the Executive Committee of the Board of Trustees at Arlington Hospital; and Chairman of the In-Depth Study Committee of the Arlington Hospital. He was a member of the State Council of Higher Education for Virginia.

His participation in organizations was not confined to Arlington County. He was a member of the Board of Directors for the Metropolitan Washington YMCA. Mr. Parker was a member of the Howard University Engineering and Architect Alumni Association, a member of the U.S. Patent Office Society, a thirty-three-degree Mason, a Shriner, a member of the Naval Reserve Policy Board, and a member of the Admissions Interview Committee at Georgetown University.

Besides the numerous awards that Mr. Parker received for his government service, he received numerous other awards, including the Howard University School of Engineering Alumni Award in 1961; the Howard University General Alumni Association Award in 1962; the Arlington Links Outstanding Citizens Award in 1968; and the Alpha Phi Civic Award in 1972.

Mr. Parker was married for forty-eight years to his wife, Lillian M. Parker. This union produced three sons: Luttrelle F. Parker Jr., Captain, United States Navy; Dr. Wendell E. Parker; and the late Marine Corps Major Raymond D. Parker. (Source: Internet Article)

Robert M. Alexander, Esq.

Robert Mossi Alexander was born to Mazie "Macy" Elizabeth Brown and Plummer Robert Alexander, Jr., in Richmond, Virginia on July 5, 1926 and was the oldest of three children. His sister, Gladys Bradley predeceased him.

Robert was drafted by the U.S. Army in 1945 while in college at Virginia Union University and served during World War II as a Sergeant in the Army Air Forces/Corps, 25th Infantry Division in the Pacific, the Philippines. He later served in the Army Reserves from 1950-1952 as a Lieutenant. After the war, Robert attended Howard University and graduated with a Bachelor of Arts Cum Laude in Political Science in 1951. He graduated from Georgetown University Law School in 1955 with a Juris Doctor degree. He passed the Virginia State Bar examination in 1954 while in law school and later completed the Certificate of Procurement of Law Program at the Judge Advocate General School, University of Virginia at Charlottesville in 1963.

In 1950, Robert married Audree Dorethea Smith of Richmond, Virginia. While Robert was a law student at Georgetown, Audree gave birth to their first son, Robert, Jr. on August 10, 1953. In 1957, Robert and Audree were blessed with twin sons, David Storrs and Charles Warren. Robert resided with his family in Arlington, Virginia for 18 years and in Alexandria for 30 years. In 2003, he moved into his last earthly home in Woodmore West subdivision of Mitchelville, Maryland where all of his housing needs were on one floor – no steps to accommodate his wife, Audree, where twenty years of debilitating Parkinson's disease destroyed her ability to walk. During their marriage, Robert and Audree travelled the world visiting 22 foreign countries.

Robert practiced law in the State of Virginia and District of Columbia over 50 years. He was a volunteer Attorney for NAACP cases for 27 years and participated in cases in which the Supreme Court of the United States barred discrimination based on race in admission to private day schools and use of recreational facilities by all owners of homes in subdivisions across the nation. He had been counsel in more than seven thousand cases in the past five decades. In several cases that he defended, his Clients were either acquitted or the charges were dismissed for lack of evidence, including a high profile spousal abuse case in the Commonwealth of Virginia.

Robert was a member of the Alpha Phi Alpha Fraternity for over 60-years, a member of the Mount Zion Baptist Church in Arlington, Virginia for over 50 years, a life member of the Arlington County NAACP, a life member of the Athenians Men's Club of Washington, DC and a member of other associations, such as the International Y's Men (YMCA) Association, the Gideons International, the Old Dominion Bar Association and the Arlington Bar Association. On June 2, 2001, the Old Dominion Bar Association awarded him the Oliver W. Hill/Samuel W. Tucker Lifetime Achievement Award for upholding and elevating the standards of honor, integrity and competence in the legal profession. In 2000, the Arlington NAACP Chapter gave Robert an "Unsung Hero" Award in recognition of legal work he handled for this organization.

Robert was married to Audree for 56 years before her passing. He is survived by his three sons, Robert M. Jr., twins David and Charles, two daughters-in-law, Carolyn Ruth Dukes and Diane Janet Howard and three grandchildren, Robert III, Lena and Janet, plus four great grandchildren, Robert IV, Jaylen, Lauryn and Isaiah. Robert passed August 2, 2014. (Excerpts from Obituary Program)

Medical Field

Roland H. Bruner, M.D.
Denise E. Bruner, M.D.

Roland H. Bruner, M.D.

Dr. Ronald Herman Bruner, who served greater Arlington for over thirty years, should not only be remembered for his commitment to medicine and generosity to the community and his patients, but also for overcoming the limitations set forth by racism and segregation in an oppressive era of American history. Dr. Bruner, the son of John Randolph Bruner and Annie Laura Dykes, was born on March 7, 1902, in Burkittsville, Maryland. In the mid-1920s, Roland Bruner left Burkittsville to attend Storer College in Harper's Ferry, West Virginia, which opened after the Civil War to educate freed slaves and then developed into a full, degree-granting college. After completing a two-year junior college program, Roland continued his education at Howard University, where he received a Bachelor of Science degree in 1928. At the time, options for prospective African American medical students were limited by racism, with only Meharry Medical College and Howard University training the majority of African American doctors.

In 1932 Dr. Bruner graduated from Howard University College of Medicine as one of twenty-four students distinguished with an internship in Freedmen's Hospital in 1932-1933. Freedmen's Hospital played a critical role in the development and training of Howard University's medical students since only six African American hospitals existed and only three white hospitals admitted African American doctors throughout the country. Dr. Bruner joined the staff of Freedmen's Hospital, following the completion of his internship.

From 1935 to 1951, he was a part-time member of the clinical faculty of Howard University's College of Medicine, serving first as a clinical assistant before his promotion to clinical instructor. There he specialized and lectured in obstetrics and gynecology.

On July 20, 1934, Dr. Bruner and his wife, Georgia Collins, purchased property in the Nauck neighborhood of Arlington, Virginia. He opened a private practice located in his house at 2018 South Glebe Road. Dr. Bruner filled a desperate need for African American physicians, as the 1930 Census listed only two practicing within Arlington County. He specialized in obstetrics, but offered general medical services to the community. Since segregation limited health care options for African American patients, Dr. Bruner often made house calls to deliver babies. The only other option for patients was to travel to Freedmen's Hospital in Washington, D.C. He was instrumental in establishing a Planned Parenthood clinic for Arlington's Department of Human Resources and in assisting African American women in acquiring birth control and contraceptives. In 1938 Dr. Bruner was the only African American doctor employed by Arlington County's Health Department in the prenatal clinics. Since African Americans were not allowed to utilize the Clarendon Health Center, Dr. Bruner held prenatal clinics in "special clinic rooms" located at Arlington's courthouse.

Dr. Bruner's notable professional achievements were only a small part of his legacy. He was an unassuming and selfless family man who committed himself to serving others, regardless of financial gain. During the Great Depression and World War II, he bartered with patients and declined payment from those who could not afford medical services. He continued to serve the Nauck community until a week before his death on May 9, 1978. Dr. Bruner's legacy is continued by his daughter, Denise Ellen Bruner, a graduate of Howard University College of Medicine, who also opened a practice in Arlington. (Courtesy of the Virginia Room, Arlington Public Library)

Denise E. Bruner, M.D.

Denise E. Bruner, M.D. is a second-generation physician practicing in Arlington, Virginia. Like her father, Dr. Herman Bruner, she graduated from Howard University College of Medicine in Washington, D.C. After completing her residency in internal medicine at D.C. General Hospital, she re-opened her late father's general medical practice in Arlington, Virginia.

Inspired by her personal struggle with weight and seeing the negative impact obesity was having on her patients' health, Dr. Bruner pursued further training in bariatric medicine, the branch of medicine that deals with the causes, prevention, and treatment of obesity. She joined the American Society of Bariatric Physicians (ASBP) in 1983, became certified by the American Board of Bariatric Medicine in 1985, and served as president of ASBP from 1999 to 2002. She was honored to become the first female fellow of the American Society of Bariatric Physicians (ASBP) in 2002. Dr. Bruner has emerged as one of the nation's leading authorities on bariatric medicine. She has helped thousands to identify, understand, and successfully manage their weight-control problems with personalized programs.

Dr. Bruner regularly lectures and is a speaker at medical education seminars for physicians and health care professionals around the world. She is a frequent guest on both television and radio programs and has been quoted in numerous publications.

Dr. Bruner lives in Arlington, Virginia, with her husband, Paul. As part of her personal weight maintenance program, Dr. Bruner regularly walks two miles a day, and when time permits, she enjoys playing golf. (Source: Internet article)

The Arts

Roberta Flack
Willie "Jamil" Garner
Iyona (Garner) Blake
Patricia Miller
Alfred A. Duncan
Betty A. Carter
Allen "Big Al" Carter

Roberta Flack

Roberta Flack lived with a musical family. She was born in Black Mountain, North Carolina, to parents Laron LeRoy (October 11, 1911–July 12, 1959) and Irene Flack (September 28, 1911–January 17, 1981) a church organist, on February 10, 1939 (1937 according to some sources) and raised in Arlington, Virginia. She first discovered the work of African American musical artists when she heard Mahalia Jackson and Sam Cooke sing in a predominantly African American Baptist church.

When Flack was nine, she started showing interest in playing the piano, and during her early teens, Flack so excelled at classical piano that Howard University awarded her a full music scholarship. By age fifteen, she entered Howard University, making her one of the youngest students ever to enroll there. She eventually changed her major from piano to voice and became an assistant conductor of the university choir. Her direction of a production of *Aida* received a standing ovation from the Howard University faculty. Flack is a member of Delta Sigma Theta sorority and was made an honorary member of Tau Beta Sigma by the Eta Delta Chapter at Howard University for her outstanding work in promoting music education.

Roberta Flack became the first African American student teacher at an all-Caucasian school near Chevy Chase, Maryland. She graduated from Howard University at nineteen and began graduate studies in music, but the sudden death of her father forced her to take a job teaching music and English for $2,800 a year in Farmville, North Carolina.

Before becoming a professional singer-songwriter, Flack taught school in Washington, D.C. at Browne Junior High and Rabaut Junior High. She also taught private piano lessons out of her home on Euclid St. N.W. During this period, her music career began to take shape on evenings and weekends at Washington, D.C. area night spots. At the Tivoli Club, she accompanied opera singers at the piano. During intermissions, she would sing blues, folk, and pop standards in a back room, accompanying herself on the piano.

Les McCann discovered Flack singing and playing jazz in a Washington nightclub. He later said on the liner notes of what would be her first album, *First Take*, "Her voice touched, tapped, trapped, and kicked every emotion I've ever known. I laughed, cried, and screamed for more...she alone had the voice." Very quickly he arranged an audition for her with Atlantic Records, during which she played forty-two songs in three hours for producer Joel Dorn. In November 1968, she recorded thirty-nine song demos in less than ten hours. Three months later, Atlantic reportedly recorded Roberta's debut album, *First Take*, in a mere ten hours.

Flack's version of "Will You Love Me Tomorrow" hit number seventy-six on the Billboard Hot 100 in 1972. Her Atlantic recordings did not sell particularly well until actor/director Clint Eastwood chose a song from *First Take*, "The

First Time Ever I Saw Your Face," for the sound track of his directorial debut, *Play Misty for Me*. It became the biggest hit of the year for 1972, spending six, consecutive weeks at number one and earning Flack a million-selling gold disc. *First Take* also went to number one and eventually sold 1.9 million copies in the United States. Eastwood, who paid two thousand dollars for the use of the song in the film, has remained an admirer and friend of Flack's ever since. It was awarded the Grammy Award for Record of the Year in 1973. In 1983 she recorded the end music to the Dirty Harry film, *Sudden Impact,* at Eastwood's request.

Roberta Flack soon began recording regularly with Donny Hathaway, scoring hits such as the Grammy-winning "Where Is the Love" (1972) and later "The Closer I Get to You" (1978), both of which were million-selling gold singles. On her own, Flack scored her second number-one hit in 1973, "Killing Me Softly with His Song," which was written by Charles Fox and Norman Gimbel and originally performed by Lori Lieberman.http://en.wikipedia.org/wiki/Roberta_Flack - cite_note-de-seret12June1997-7 Flack and Hathaway recorded several duets together, including two LPs, until Hathaway's 1979 death.

In 1999 a star with Flack's name was placed on Hollywood's Walk of Fame. That same year, she gave a concert tour in South Africa, to which the final performance was attended by President Nelson Mandela. In 2010 she appeared on the 52nd Annual Grammy Awards, singing a duet of "Where Is the Love" with Maxwell.

Flack is a member of the Artist Empowerment Coalition, which advocates the right of artists to control their creative properties. She is also a spokesperson for the American Society for the Prevention of Cruelty to Animals. Her appearance in commercials for the ASPCA featured "The First Time Ever I Saw Your Face." In the Bronx section of New York City, the Hyde Leadership Chart School's after-school music program is called the "Roberta Flack School of Music" and is in partnership with Flack, who founded the school, which provides free music education to underprivileged students.

According to a DNA analysis, she descended, mainly, from people of Cameroon. (Source: Wikepedia.com)

Willie "Jamil" Garner

Willie "Jamil" Garner was born, raised, and educated in Arlington, Virginia, public schools. After graduating from Wakefield High School, he then went on to graduate from Shenandoah Conservatory of Shenandoah University. He holds a Bachelors of Fine Arts in Musical Theatre. While growing up, theater has always been a passion of his.

He started his theatrical career by performing around the Nauck community with such acts as the Arlington Youth Street Theatre (AYST), the Dominion Stage, and most recently, The Arlington Players. Some of his memorable performance credits include, *A Chorus Line* (Richie), *Hairspray* (Seaweed J. Stubbs), *Damn Yankees* (Henry/Baseball Player), *Ragtime, South Pacific, Curtain's, Oliver, Dreamgirls, and The Color Purple.*

Outside of the stage, Willie is the Assistant Director of Living Water Dance Ministry at Macedonia Baptist Church in Arlington, Virginia. Among other things, he has a passion for teaching, as is evidenced by his travel to such areas as Pottstown Middle School in Pottstown, Pennsylvania, where he teaches four days a week at the Theatre Workshop. Currently Willie is an assistant monitor at Kenmore Middle School and Ashlawn Elementary School. Willie hopes to one day be in the classroom, teaching special education students the fundamentals of performing arts. His lifetime goal is to give back to the community that helped nurture and support the foundation laid before him by his parents and church family.

"Dancing can reveal all the mystery that music conceals." - Charles Baudelaire (Source: Willie "Jamil" Garner)

Iyona Garner Blake

Iyona Blake is a singer, actor, recitalist, vocal coach, and music instructor. Iyona Blake's great adventure began in Arlington, Virginia. Born and raised in the midst of a musical family, her unique gifts were recognized and nurtured early on. If you know Iyona Blake, you know Iyona Blake can sing. For her music has always been more passion than past-time.

Over the years, Iyona Blake has had many opportunities to share and develop her gifts. Through much hard work, dedication, and grace, she has endeavored to make the most of each one.

Notably, she received a vocal performance diploma from Duke Ellington School of the Arts in Washington, D.C. She later earned a Bachelor's in Voice Performance with a concentration in opera from Shenandoah Conservatory at Shenandoah University (S.U.) in Winchester, Virginia. While at S.U., Iyona Blake competed in and won numerous, first-place singing competitions, directed the college gospel choir, and was awarded several, leading operatic roles.

Having been nourished by years of classical training and discipline, Iyona Blake grew from exceptional music student to exceptional music teacher. Her signature teaching style and passion for sharing the wonder of music proved an excellent fit for both the Arlington and Fairfax County Virginia school systems. As a vocal and choral concepts instructor, Iyona Blake's unique ability to connect and relate through music allowed her to effectively teach students on all grade-levels, including those with special needs and disabilities.

In the spring of 2013, Iyona Blake performed "My Favorite Things," a sixty-minute recital of her favorite art songs, arias, spirituals, and musical theater repertoire. Iyona has also been seen on stage, Off Broadway, in the musical, *Soul on Fire,* as Gabriel and Eva Mae; a Griot in the *Christmas Gift;* Desiree/Celina in *Breast in Show*, a breast cancer musical; Fats Waller's *Ain't Misbehavin'* as Armelia McQueen; and Langston Hughes in *Black Nativity*. Iyona's operatic roles include the Countess (*The Marriage of Figaro*), Magda Sorel (*The Consul*), Liu (*Turandot*), Marie (*The Bartered Bride),* and Bess *(Porgy and Bess)*. She has made solo appearances performing "Ave Maria" in the Kennedy Center's Concert Hall in Washington, D.C. and has been featured as the encore soloist with the National Symphony Orchestra.

In 2012 Iyona made a T.V. and concert appearance with Academy and Tony award-winning Glen Hansard. In the summer of 2012, Iyona joined an impressive ensemble of nine, professional singers on a cultural envoy to Cairo, Egypt, representing the United States (one of twelve countries) in an international festival of sacred music and chanting. In 2008 she was also blessed to have completed her gospel solo project entitled *"Released."*

Currently Iyona Blake is a general music teacher at the Montessori School of Northern Virginia, a voice professor in the theater arts department at Howard University, a sought-after private, voice instructor and coach, and a voice clinician at vocal music seminars and workshops throughout the East Coast. Most importantly Iyona is married to Billy Blake and has two children, Caeli and Mathias. (Source: Iyona Blake)

Patricia Miller

Patricia Miller is an internationally acclaimed operatic and concert mezzo-soprano. She is also a highly respected voice teacher and music educator. A university professor, artist-teacher, and master class clinician, her talent and commitment to opera education have taken her all over the world. She is Director of Vocal Studies at George Mason University and serves on the Opera Panel of the National Endowment for the Arts.

Miss Miller has appeared in leading, operatic roles with the San Francisco Opera, the Houston Grand Opera, and the Dallas, Detroit, Miami, Denver, Orange County (CA), Los Angeles, and New York City Opera companies. She made her European debut with the Basel Stadttheater (State Theater) Opera, in Basel, Switzerland, as Isabella in *Rossini's L'Italiana in Algeri*, and has since performed in opera and concert in Paris, Geneva, Lyon, Montpellier, Lisbon, Munich, Bonn, Frankfort, Melbourne, Bogota, Calgary, Berlin, Moscow, Kiev, Verona, and Tokyo. She has sung the title role in Bizet's *Carmen* with opera companies throughout Europe, Australia, and North and South America, and she was chosen by the great British director, Peter Brook, to sing the title role in his highly acclaimed production of *La Tragedie de Carmen* in Munich, Milan, Pompeii, Verona, and Tokyo.

Miller's vocal artistry is described as "captivating" (*San Francisco Chronicle*), "passionate and sensuous" (*Il Giornale di Napoli/Italy*), "powerful and moving" (*Le Monde/Paris*), and "rich and beautiful" (*Opera/London*). In a recent performance at Lisner Auditorium, the *Washington Post* described Miss Miller's voice as "creamy, expressive, and ideal" for the *Brahms Rhapsody*. From a Washington, D.C. recital performance, critic Joseph McClellan (*Washington Post*) wrote, "Miller's voice is deep, rich in tonal beauty and power, and comfortable in a wide range of styles." From an April 2003 performance of the *Verdi Requiem*, Joe Banno (*Washington Post*) wrote, "Patricia Miller brought a real sense of Verdian drama to the score's big moments with her powerhouse mezzo."

In February 2004, at Old Town Hall in Fairfax, Virginia, Miss Miller was honored by the Fairfax Virginia Commission on the Arts and given an Honorary Alumnae Artist Award from the Washington, D.C. Alumnae chapter of the Sigma Alpha Iota International Music Fraternity, Inc. In March 2004, she received the Sojourner Truth Award from George Mason University and the African American Studies and GMU Women's Center for her commitment to the musical arts and arts education. In 2008 Miss Miller was named Distinguished University Professor of Music by the Board of Visitors at George Mason University.

Miss Miller is in high demand as a competition adjudicator for The International Voice Competition (National Association of Arts & Letters, Washington, D.C.); the National Symphony Young Soloist's Competition (Kennedy Center); the Jack Kent Cooke undergraduate and graduate Fellowship Awards; the NAACP National Voice Competition; the Peabody Conservatory Voice Competition; the Annapolis Opera Competition; the National Association of Teachers of Singing (NATS); and NAATSA regional and state competitions, among many others.

Miss Miller's distinguished biography is listed in *Who's Who in America* (2003-2010), *Who's Who in American Education* (2005-2009), *Who's Who Among American Women* (2008-09) and *Who's Who in the World* (2008-2010).

Miss Miller is a graduate of Boston University and the New England Conservatory. As a Fulbright Scholar, she received an Artist diploma from the Accademia di Santa Cecilia in Rome, Italy. She attributes her success to music education early on in her life and to outstanding mentor-teachers throughout her life, including: her parents, Robert and Bernice Miller (Arlington, Virginia); Maestro Luigi Ricci (Rome, Italy); Gladys Miller Zachareff (New England Conservatory); Eleanor Steber (New England Conservatory/New York City); Peter Brook (Paris, France); Shirlee Emmons (New York City); Richard Miller (Salzburg, Austria); and Mattiwilda Dobbs (Arlington, Virginia).

Miss Miller is distinguished professor of music and is an artist-in-residence at George Mason University where, in addition to the aforementioned Director of Vocal Studies, she is also Artistic Director of the Mason Opera Theater. She has been a *Reader's Digest* sponsored artist-in-residence at Lafayette College; a professor of voice at the University of Missouri in Columbia, Missouri; and a professor of voice at the Oberlin College Conservatory of Music in Oberlin, Ohio. (Source: Wikipedia)

Alfred A. Duncan

Alfred Antonio Duncan is a widely sought-after local talent, having created a niche as an on-stage and radio host and as a lead vocalist for a nationally touring band.

Reared in Prince George's County, Maryland, Mr. Duncan graduated from Forestville High School in 1993. At Forestville Mr. Duncan was president of The Black Male Achievement Group and a percussionist in the award-winning Forestville marching band. He also played on Forestville's then-championship basketball team.

Upon graduating from Forestville, Mr. Duncan went on to Shenandoah University in Winchester, Virginia, where he played point guard on the men's basketball team. In 1995 Shenandoah's team, with significant contributions from Mr. Duncan, had a record season and competed in the first round of the NCAA Tournament. Mr. Duncan graduated from Shenandoah in 1999 with a Bachelor of Arts in Mass Communications, with a minor concentration in religion.

After college Mr. Duncan returned to the Washington, D.C. area, where he held various jobs at prestigious companies, including: IBM, Dewberry & Davis, and Verizon. He worked as a promotional assistant with WKYS 93.9, where he also created and performed on-air parodies and show introductions.

Throughout the years, Mr. Duncan never neglected his first love: music. He was initially best known for his singing, often performing at talent shows and traveling around the nation with the award-winning NAACP Youth Choir, Images of Unity. As he matured in music, Mr. Duncan found that he was also gifted in rhyming and writing raps.

Now Mr. Duncan is known across the United States as "Black Boo," the lead vocalist for the band, Mambo Sauce. He is coined one of the most talented lyricists and song writers in the D.C. area. Mambo Sauce, known for their hit songs, "Welcome to D.C." and "Miracles," recently returned from their first, national tour with famed international reggae artist, SOJA. Mambo Sauce successfully brought the original D.C. sound of go-go to sold-out crowds in cities like Los Angeles, Portland, Dallas, New Orleans, and Chicago, to name just a few.

Mr. Duncan has been lending his talent and personality in other aspects of the entertainment field, as well. He is currently the co-host of the Up and Up Open Mic—the mecca of great talent in the DMV—which was named the "Best Open Mic in Washington, D.C." by the *Washington Post*.

Mr. Duncan is also popular among Washington Redskins fans for his viral Redskins-themed remixes played on WPGC 95.5 and Comcast Sportsnet.

In his spare time, Mr. Duncan enjoys giving back to the youth, playing basketball, and spending time with "his boys": his son, Blake and nephew, Chauncey. He proudly lives by the motto, "Work ain't hard," and uses his music and the stage to encourage people everywhere to never stop pursuing their dreams. (Source: Alfred A. Duncan)

Allen "Big Al" Carter

Painter Compulsive Defied Stylistic Trends

By Matt Schudel, *Washington Post* staff writer, Sunday, January 11, 2009
Allen "Big Al" Carter, here in 2006, painted obsessively, but was never fully comfortable in the world of art galleries. (David Peterson, Washington Post)

Allen D. "Big Al" Carter, an immensely productive artist who defied stylistic trends and commercial expectations to pursue his singular vision on no one's terms but his own, died on December 18 of complications from diabetes at Virginia Hospital Center. He was sixty-one and lived in Alexandria.

Mr. Carter had exhibited his works widely since the 1970s, often receiving ecstatic reviews from critics, but he was never fully comfortable with the world of art galleries and patrons. Instead, he spent thirty years teaching in alternative schools in Arlington County while compulsively drawing and painting at home.

His work is in the permanent collection of the Corcoran Gallery of Art and, during the past three years, was featured in museum exhibitions in North Carolina and Minnesota. He was also a photographer early in his career, and his photographs of elderly relatives in rural Virginia were featured at the Alexandria Black History Museum in 2007.

Mr. Carter sold some of his artwork to friends and collectors, but he was reluctant to part with much of it. Working feverishly at all hours of the day and night, he amassed a cache of thousands of paintings, drawings, and collages that varied from wall-size murals to miniature watercolors that could fit in the palm of his hand. Most of his art has never been seen in public.

"He is a particular type of Washington artist," Mary Battiata wrote in the *Washington Post Magazine* in 2006, "someone who was understood by peers to have the promise to make it in New York, but who for one reason or another—temperament, taste, fear, arrogance, or some combination—decided to stay here and fashion a different, quieter career and life."

Mr. Carter stood 6 feet 3 inches, weighed 340 pounds, and possessed a gregarious, larger-than-life personality that made him an unforgettable character to many who knew him. He was known to one and all—including himself—as "Big Al" or just "Big."

He was sometimes perceived as an unschooled "outsider" artist but, in fact, he had a solid education in art history and technique.

"Carter's art is protean, large-hearted, never prissy," *Washington Post* critic Paul Richard wrote of a 1985 exhibition at a local gallery. "Warmth pours from the walls. To walk into the gallery is to accept Big Al's embrace."

A 1990 *New York Times* review said his paintings "suggest boundless, uncontrollable freedom . . . [a] complex world of reality, dream, and art."

Despite such acclaim, Mr. Carter did not allow his artwork to be shown in the country's art capital, New York, where he could have found greater renown and remuneration. He thought the commissions charged by art galleries were too high, and he broke with his longtime Washington gallery more than five years ago.

Much to the annoyance of curators and collectors, Mr. Carter did not date his paintings and offered only vague hints at when they were made. He painted on canvas, T.V. trays, lampshades, boat rudders, and home-movie screens, and he incorporated musical instruments, brushes, wood, and other objects into works. He often used house paint and rummaged through trash bins behind art stores for half-used tubes of oil and acrylic paint.

He marched freely across the borderlines of artistic styles, combining abstraction and swirls of pure energy with recognizable landscapes and portraits. His strong lines reminded some viewers of modern-art pioneer, Georges Rouault. Other critics likened his multimedia constructions to those of Robert Rauschenberg, but Mr. Carter thought such comparisons slighted his originality.

He often depicted themes from African American life and was exhibited alongside such renowned African American artists as Romare Bearden, but Mr. Carter resisted racial labels and preferred to be called simply an "American artist."

His work sometimes featured animals, nudes, pop culture images, or topical references to veterans and warfare. He also had an unexhibited series of fifty paintings based on the Holocaust.

"I paint poor and rich people and their relationships in this society," he told the *Virginian-Pilot* newspaper in 1997. "I paint the hungry, the homeless, war veterans, children, the powerful, and the powerless. I depict pain, joy, contradictions, hope, and despair."

Allen Dester Carter was born on June 29, 1947, in Washington and grew up in Arlington (Nauck). His parents had a church in Gainesville that Mr. Carter attended three times a week. He played football at Wakefield High School but was devoted to art from an early age, despite his parents' misgivings. In case he awoke in the middle of the night with an urge to draw, he kept sheets of paper beside his bed.

"I couldn't stop drawing," he told the *Post* three years ago. "Anything that was white I had to draw on it."

His only prolonged absence from the Washington region came when he moved to Ohio to attend the Columbus College of Art and Design, from which he graduated in 1970. He returned to Northern Virginia and taught at three centers for continuing and alternative education in Arlington County. In the 1990s, he moved to Fredericksburg and loaded freight trucks for a few years before moving to Alexandria and returning to his old teaching job. He retired in 2007.

At the end of his teaching day, Mr. Carter returned to his cramped house to take up his brush. He painted with astonishing speed and sometimes completed a large canvas in less than an hour. In 1982 he painted a ten-by-twenty-five-foot mural on a building on Seventh Street N.W. in two days.

Mr. Carter spent most of his life near Washington and did not like to travel far, except to catch fish or hunt deer with a bow and arrow. He went only as far as he could go by foot or in his undependable van. He refused to board a train, an airplane, or a boat.

"All these things add up to an artist who was driven by his internal compass," said Steven Tepper, a Vanderbilt University official who had known Mr. Carter since the early 1990s. "We all wonder what a true artist is like. Once you meet him, you have the answer to that question."

Mr. Carter's marriage to Mae I. Carter ended in divorce. Survivors include his two daughters, Flora Stone and Cecilia Carter, both of Newport News; a sister, Shirley Chestnut of Alexandria; a brother, Alford Carter of Manassas; and two granddaughters.

"I've never been to Paris or any of those places," Mr. Carter told the *Post* in 1984, "but all you've got to do is just set up and paint. Art just comes naturally. You just put it down on paper. You've got to keep rolling…just keep on rolling." (Source: Internet)

Betty Angela Carter

Betty Carter is the daughter to the proud parents of the late Mattie F. and Leo E. Carter. She was born on September 5, 1958, in Washington, D.C. at Columbia Hospital for Women. During that time, even though her parents resided in Arlington, Virginia, all African American pregnant mothers had to go to Washington, D.C. to give birth. They were not allowed to go the hospitals in Arlington.

She had one brother, Leslie E. Carter. Both kids attended Drew Elementary School. Betty loved music. As early as the third grade, the music teacher informed her parents that Betty had a special gift for singing. She joined Macedonia Baptist Church in 1969 and sang with the Bells of Joy (a children choir). She led a song and got a standing ovation from the congregation. At the age of fourteen, Betty joined a group called the Young People's Choir of Macedonia Baptist Church. She asked her dad about singing gospel music. He told her to listen to Mahalia Jackson, The Caravans, and James Cleveland. He even made Betty sit in a chair and memorize all the words to the Dionne Warwick songs," Do you know the way to San Jose" and "Alfie" to broaden her singing style. Her father, Leo E. Carter, was a great musician in the Metropolitan area. He performed at WUST, D.C. radio stations, and various churches all over the East Coast. Leo played for the Virginia Harmonizers, the Swan Silver Tones, and the Mighty Clouds of Joy. Betty traveled with him when she was not attending school. She enjoyed watching her father perform. He played the bass guitar and sang bass. While attending Wakefield High School, she got the role as Reno Sweeney in the Musical, *Anything Goes*. She was the first African American to have a leading role ever at Wakefield High School. Betty went on to attend Norfolk State University on full scholarship. She was the recipient of the Nauck Citizens Association Award in 1976. She majored in music in media. She participated in various activities at Norfolk State University. She was a lead soloist for the NSU Jazz Band, member of the Norfolk State Players, member of Delta Sigma Theta, Inc. (Omicron Epsilon Chapter), and host of the campus cable show, *Norfolk State Highlights*.

After graduation she came back to Arlington and married Bryant Mercer. She later divorced and returned to singing. She has performed with Arena Stage, the Spirit of Washington, the Lincoln Theater, the D.C. Black Rep Theater, the Atlas Theatre, and the Bobby Jones Gospel Show. She has opened for such musical groups as Roy Ayes, Tramaine Hawkins, Edwin Birdsong, Mother's finest, and many others. She sang for the 9-11 tragedy at the Air Force Memorial and Arlington Cemetery. She has produced her first musical production entitled, *You Better Ask Somebody*. "I have a great passion for the Arts and I know this is a great tool for communication." (Source: Betty A. Carter)

Patricia Velator Smith

Patricia Velator Smith was born to parents Walter and Edna Smith. Velator was born in Fairfax, Virginia, at Ft. Belvoir's Dwight Hospital. She is the first child of four children. She was raised in Arlington, Virginia, attending Charles Drew Elementary School, Kemper and Hoffman Boston, Thomas Jefferson Middle School, and Wakefield High School. She attended Northern Virginia College, Gallaudet University, and Trinity College. Velator worked at the Arlington County Alcohol and Drug Program, Offender Aid and Restoration, and at the Arlington County Department of Parks and Recreation. Just Before retiring, she worked as a family support worker in Alexandria for Northern Virginia Family Services. During her employment there, she was chosen to sit on a panel with the former First Lady Hillary Clinton.

Velator is the proud parent of one daughter, Adia, and four grandchildren, Jasmine, Prince, Bishop, and Duke. She is an active member of the Macedonia Baptist Church of Arlington, Virginia. In 2000 she became physically challenged. Although confined to a wheelchair, she continues to be an active member at her church and in the community. Velator is a story creator and poet. She combines music, dance movements, and sign language in her creative storytelling. She has traveled throughout the United States and London, England, performing. She self-published a poetry book, *A Caged Butterfly Freed*. She is presently revising the book. She volunteers monthly at the Potomac Nursing Home in Arlington, where she reads and creates poetic stories with the residents. She also can be found performing at schools and other social events. She feels her poetic stories are God's work. She trusts fully in God. (Source: Velator Smith)

Company Executives

Kenneth M. (Kenny) Taylor
Clifton N. West

Kenneth M. (Kenny) Taylor

Kenneth M. Taylor, son of Dr. Alfred and Delores Taylor, is a native of Washington, D.C. A graduate of Calvin Coolidge High School, he was introduced to instrumental music while attending Rabaut Jr. High School and continued as a member of the brass section of the Coolidge concert and marching band, while simultaneously serving as pianist for the school's award-winning gospel choir and musician on staff at Macedonia Baptist Church in Arlington, Virginia, where he served for over thirty-eight years. While at Rabaut Jr. High School, he studied music under Roberta Flack. He also studied at the Modern School of Music and Sewell's Conservatory of Music.

After graduating from high school, Kenny attended Florida A&M University to study music, but he found that his primary interest was retail. He then enrolled in and graduated from the Barbizon School of Fashion Merchandising. For the next, few years, he excelled in the retail industry, quickly rising to upper management positions with the Ups & Down/Proving Ground Corporation based out of Dearborn, Michigan. In 1980 he was transferred to Michigan and resided there for over a year until he was transferred back to this region to oversee the top, five stores in the chain.

Shortly afterwards Kenny was hired by Kay Jewelers/Black, Starr & Frost. Working in the corporate offices in Old Towne Alexandria, he traveled extensively throughout the country to implement and train store management in the operation of the new, point-of-sale computer system. Once the new system was fully implemented, he remained at Kay Jewelers as national display coordinator, creating and implementing the monthly display campaigns while personally overseeing the opening of new stores.

He later resumed his duties at Macedonia as a church musician. At the urging of the Northern Virginia chapter of the NAACP, he formed a youth community choir known as Images of Unity. Under his direction, the youth travelled extensively, ministering in Florida, Connecticut, Atlanta, Cincinnati, New York, up and down the Eastern seaboard, and points west, including Los Angeles, California. The group enjoyed numerous television appearances and high-profile platforms to include Bobby Jones Gospel.

Having worked the gamut of retail positions, in 1998 he consolidated his love of gospel music and retail when he was hired as mid-Atlantic representative for Atlanta International Records (Air Gospel). He was eventually relocated to Atlanta, Georgia, where he was promoted to national promotions director, serving until 2005 when the company was sold to a Jackson, Mississippi-based company.

Opting not to relocate from Atlanta to Jackson, he returned to the D.C. area and formed his own company, Teemade Promotions, a full-service marketing and promotions firm and has been continually building its brand in the gospel music industry.

Working as consultant for many of the major gospel labels, he has guided the careers of top-charting artists, including: Dottie Peoples, Earnest Pugh, Maurette Brown Clark, Luther Barnes, Lisa Page Brooks, Wilmington Chester

Mass Choir, Damon Little, Bubby Fann, Evelyn Turrentine Agee, Keith Pringle, the late Reverend Timothy Wright, and Reverend F.C. Barnes, just to name a few.

A noted event planner, July 2013 marked his fourteenth annual Artist Showcase at the Gospel Music Workshop of America. The event has grown to be one of the most anticipated events during the music conference. As chief marketing officer for the New Orleans-based Versatile Entertainment, the company produces Bobby Jones Gospel in New Orleans and Praise Fest, a growing New Orleans fall community festival.

In 2007 Kenny gained the distinction of being one of the top ten independent consultants in the U.S.A. by The Gospel Music Industry Round-Up, an annual publication that is the "go-to" manual for anything pertaining to the gospel music industry, such as record labels, artist contact info, print, television, and Internet media. Now enjoying six years on the list, he continues to remain active in that arena.

Presently on staff at the Second Baptist Church in Suitland, Maryland, the Evergreen Baptist Church in Washington, D.C., and the Forcey Memorial Church in Silver Spring, Maryland, he takes pride in the fact that as extensive as his travel schedule can be as a gospel music executive, he manages to get back to the area by Sunday to satisfy his first love, that of a church musician. (Source: Kenneth M. Taylor)

Clifton N. (Skeeter) West

Clifton West is a fourth generation Washingtonian who grew up in Arlington County (Green Valley). He was the youngest of three children born to the late Clifton N. West and Thaddenia Hayes West. He is also the great grandson of William A. Rowe, one of the first Arlington, Virginia, superintendents. He attended Kemper/Kemper Annex Elementary School, Francis Jr. High School, and Dunbar High School, where he started the first drill team and was the winner of the competitive drill each of his three years there. He was star in indoor and outdoor track in well as cross country. After high school h went to Howard University where he was a star of the Penn Relays and the Evening Star meets and many others. He did further study at George Washington University in Washington, D.C., and at the Department of Agriculture Graduate and National Institute of Health Graduate Schools. He also has received training from Brooke Army Medical Technology School in Houston, Texas, and worked at Hyland Lab Management, Coulter Hematology, Technician Chemistry, Hycel Chemistry, Roche Chemistry, Olympus Chemistry, and Virginia Chemistry.

He served in the United States Air Force in France and was stationed at various hospital labs. While in France, he also played basketball for the USAF professional team, playing against professional teams in Europe.

He has worked at St. Elizabeth's Hospital and set up the medical laboratory at NASA. During his tenure at Berkley Medical Labs and Miles Laboratories, he set up medical labs in the mid-Atlantic area, from North Carolina to New Jersey.

Mr. West is currently the owner and president/CEO of B&W Stat Laboratory, Inc., providing service to the District of Columbia drug treatment programs and many other local organizations. He also serves on the Board of Directors and Health Advisory Committee at Leisure World of Maryland.

In 1963 B&W Labs was the first laboratory to set up routine medical laboratory testing for physicians in the Washington, D.C. area by providing physicians with collection samples, specimen pick-ups, immediate (STAT) testing, and results within one day. He developed methodology and instrument testing for toxicology procedures. Because of the precision, specificity, and sensitivity, the B&W was awarded the first drug court contract in the District of Columbia's Superior Court. This was the first court laboratory within the United States for the purpose of testing for substance abuse and/or dependency. His innovation of drug testing facilitated a judge's decision to send a defendant to drug treatment rather than jail. He was awarded the Outstanding Small Business Award for the years 1996 and 2002. He was also awarded the Excellence in Sciences Services-Masons. Mr. West was the founder and president of Lower Georgia Avenue Business and Professional Association, the founder of Georgia Avenue Day (nine years), and the vice president of the Washington, D.C. Drug Prevention Association. He spends his leisure time playing golf and holds memberships in the Pro-Duffers Golf Association, the Argyle Country Club, the University of Maryland golf course, and Leisure World. (Source: Clifton N. West)

Educators

Karen Denise Taylor
Alverna Virginia Mackley Miller
Delores Smith Taylor
Miss Lillian S. Smackum
Lottie Burke Bellamy
Marie Gee
Dr. Pamela Denise Preston

Karen Denise Taylor

Karen Denise Taylor was born in Washington, D.C. on October 3, 1964, and moved to Arlington, Virginia, in 1994. She is the daughter of Dr. Alfred O. and Delores S. Taylor. She has one brother, Kenneth M. (Kenny) Taylor, a gospel music promoter and the proud mother of three sons: Kourtnay Michael Taylor, Aaron JaRootz Steele, and Ariel Garrett Steele. She also cherishes two granddaughters, Miya Alexis and Maliah Nicole McCurdy.

Karen attended Keene Elementary, Notre Dame Academy, and McKinley Technical High School in Washington, D.C. and later studied at the University of the District of Columbia and at the Northern Virginia Community College. Karen also holds a certificate from the Washington Beauty Academy as a cosmetologist.

Karen has been employed as a special education paraprofessional since 1996 at Gunston Middle School, where she is affectionately referred to by the students as "Ms. Karen." She is an avid reader and spends most of her leisure time pursuing this as her preferred hobby. (Source: Karen D. Taylor)

Alverna Virginia Mackley Miller

Alverna Virginia Mackley Miller is the oldest daughter of the late Reverend Dr. Aaron Mackley and Deaconess Mamie Mackley Brown. Although born and raised in Washington, D.C., she was raised primarily in Arlington, Virginia (Green Valley). She attended Kemper School, Drew Elementary, Shaw Junior High School, and Cardozo Senior High School in Washington, D.C. Following graduation from Cardozo High School, she attended Morgan State College, later receiving a degree in health and physical education from the former District of Columbia Teachers College. A master's degree was conferred by the George Washington University with an emphasis on therapeutic recreation and gerontology. Advanced studies were pursued at the University of Virginia, Maryland University, the Catholic University of America, and Hofstra University.

After thirty years in the Arlington County, Virginia, Public School System, she taught personal and family living, health, and physical education in the District of Columbia at Carter G. Woodson and Paul Junior High Schools and the Iona Whipper School for Pregnant School Age Girls. Some of her work in Arlington County Schools included initiating a conflict mediation program; developing teacher training programs in health education that offered graduate credit coursework; reviewing pre-publication manuscripts for Allyn & Bacon Publishers in human sexuality, substance abuse, and AIDS (grades K-12); and organizing the Arlington County Division of the Commonwealth for Drug Rehabilitation and Education (CADRE). Selected commendations include:

Worked as a secretary to the Board of Directors of the REDEEM Community Development Corporation

- Worked as an administrator of the First Baptist Church of Deanwood's Community Upreach Center
- Earned a master's degree in 1977 from George Washington University, with an emphasis on therapeutic recreation and gerontology
- Served on the board of directors for the American Heart Association, American Cancer Society, and the American Lung Association
- Retired from the Arlington County School System after thirty years
- Resigned from the District of Columbia School System in 1970
- Organized the Arlington Virginia Division of the Commonwealth Alliance for Drug Rehabilitation and Education (CORE)
- Successfully completed SERC Training for a Drug-Free Community
- Assisted in developing curricula for the Drug Prevention Program and Family Life Education Program for the Arlington County Public School System
- Consulted with the United States Department of Education on the selection of substance abuse audio/visual materials
- Served on the board of directors of the Washington Area Council on Alcohol and Drug Abuse (WACADA)
- Reviewed substance abuse and human sexuality manuscripts for Allyn & Bacon Publications (National)
- Developed and presented a workshop, "Problems Confronting Youth Today," at the annual conference of the Progressive National Baptist Convention, Inc. and the Progressive National Baptist Christian Institute in Washington, D.C.
- Assisted teachers with the implementation of substance abuse prevention programs
- Initiated conflict education program for Arlington County Public Schools; chaired the health and physical education department and directed the intramural sports program
- Coordinated County-wide health and physical education programs for grades K-12
- Chaired the health and physical education department and directed the intramural sports program
- Developed a teacher training program that offered graduate credit coursework in health education and workshops in cancer prevention and nutrition
- Planned and coordinated teacher training workshops in the areas of health and physical education and substance abuse education
- Assisted with the revision of the secondary health curriculum for the *AIDS Instructional Guide* and chapters on nutrition and health
- Chaired the Virginia Visiting Committee on Health and Physical Education
- Presented the Creative Teacher Award at the District of Columbia Public Schools

Alverna is married to Henry Miller (October 1956), and they are the proud parents of Reverend Dr. Paula Miller-Lester and the grandparents of Allen Corde Lester. Mrs. Miller is actively involved as a member of the First Baptist Church of Deanwood in the following ministries: Andrew J. Allen Sunday Church School; Barnabas HIV/AIDS Community Outreach Center; the S.M.A.R.T. Moves Ministry (founder); and the REDEEM Community Development Corporation. (Source: Alverna Miller)

Delores Smith Taylor

Delores Smith Taylor, the daughter of Van H. and Beatrice A. Smith, was born on March 8, 1936, in Washington, D.C. She attended Kemper and Kemper Annex Elementary Schools, where she graduated in the second class from Kemper Annex. Among her classmates was Roberta Flack, the acclaimed singer. After leaving Kemper, she attended Shaw Junior High School and Cardozo High School, both in Washington, D.C. She furthered her educational training at the Washington Technical Institute, where she was the recipient of an associate degree in child development. She later received her B.A. degree from Federal City College (now the University of the District of Columbia) in early childhood education. While studying for her associate's degree, she was hired by the D.C. Public School System as an educational aide, where she served until being elevated to a math resource teacher upon the receipt of her bachelor's degree. She served in this position for over twenty years, until her retirement in 1996.

Delores has been active in the Nauck community and its activities for most of her life. She was a member of the first Girl Scout troop, which was established by Mrs. Lillian Green, and she received numerous accolades for her community work. She also served as one of the den mother's for Cub Scout Pack 589 which, at that time, was recognized as one of Arlington's largest Cub Scout packs, along with Boy Scout Troop 589. She was a charter member of the Y's Menettes, a service club for the Veteran's Memorial YMCA and the Divettes Golf Club. She holds membership in the Arlington Branch of the NAACP, the Nauck Civic Association, and the Northern Virginia Alumnae Chapter of Delta Sigma Theta Sorority, Inc. She served as the President of the Omega Wives, an auxiliary to the Omega Psi Phi Fraternity, Inc., for over ten years.

She has been an active member at the Macedonia Baptist Church for more than sixty years. The Church was founded in 1908 by her grandparents, Bonder and Amanda Johnson. Over the years, she has been a member of the junior choir and the gospel chorus. She presently serves in the Deaconess and Recreation Ministries of the Church.

She has been married to Dr. Alfred O. Taylor, Jr., for over sixty-two years, and together they have two children: Kenneth M. (Kenny), a gospel keyboardist and CEO of Teemade Productions, and Karen Denise, a special education para-professional with Arlington County schools. They are also blessed with three grandsons, Kourtnay, Aaron, and Ariel, and two great-granddaughters, Miya and Maliah. (Source: Delores S. Taylor)

Miss Lillian S. Smackum (Principal Kemper School)

It is safe to say that the pupils of Drew-Kemper School will not remember the name or recall the faces of all of their teachers. But it is equally certain that there are some they will never forget. Among these is Miss Smackum, who will be remembered by countless boys and girls, for she struck a responsive chord within all who were fortunate enough to be a pupil in any of her classes. Miss Smackum was the principal of Kemper for years, and she was the first administrative principal of Drew-Kemper School. During her years as a teacher and principal, she was unexcelled in her ability to do a splendid job at molding the minds, morals, and personalities of the pupils and stressing the development of good habits and personality traits. Because of the great influence of Miss Smackum's teaching, many Drew-Kemper pupils are able to take their rightful place as useful members of society. (Source: Internet)

Lottie Burke Bellamy

Lottie Burke Bellamy was an exceptional parent, a gifted musician, and an outstanding citizen. Mrs. Bellamy had a passion for the arts and knowledge of music as a pianist, organist, and musical director for the Macedonia Baptist Church in Arlington, Virginia, for over thirty years. During those years, she mentored her music students and provided private piano lessons at affordable rates. One of her students was Ms. Roberta Flack, a renowned, accomplished performer and recording artist. Mrs. Bellamy always considered it a privilege and a civic responsibility to give back to her community. (Excerpted from article from the Lottie Burke Bellamy Achievement Scholarship)

Marie Gee

Marie Gee was born on a warm, spring Day in April to two, hard-working people who relocated here from Raleigh, North Carolina. She has always been a busy person who uses up all her nervous energy. She started school at George Washington Carver in northeast Washington. In the second or third grade, she transferred to the Arlington County Public Schools. She remembers climbing the rocky, tree-lined hill to reach Kemper School. As she advanced in her education, she was assigned to Drew School. She could stand at the top of the second-floor stairs and see Green Valley Drug Store and her church, Lomax AME Zion. Mrs. Saunders was her school nurse, and Mr. Maltrie was the principal. A few years before she left Drew, a new, primary wing was added to the back of the building. Some of the teachers there included Ms. Marie Cooley, Mrs. Catherine Ross, and Mrs. Elizabeth Hazel.

She lived in the Dunbar homes on Kemper Road. She resided in the row directly behind the "Center." The Center was a multi-purpose room where dances were frequently held on Friday nights. Many a night she pressed her nose to the glass, and listened to the music that filled the night air. When she was growing up, she was not allowed in the Green Valley Drug Store. Beside the Green Valley Drug Store there was a club called the Sugar Bowl. It seemed that every Friday night there was a fight or stabbing at that establishment, so she only walked that way on Sunday morning, on her way to Sunday school.

Shirlington was a thriving business district with an elegant dress shop, Jelleff's; a department store, Lansburg; a Firestone, which took care of automotive needs; a drug store, Drug Fair; and a restaurant, Hot Shoppe, which shared corners where the traffic light hangs. The largest business in the area that hired many men from the Nauck community was Cherner's Lincoln/Mercury Dealer. This was a striking sight as one viewed the shiny cars in the elevated, well-lit showroom. Shirlington Cleaners and Aristo Cleaners kept people looking good, and a Highs Ice Cream Parlor satisfied their sweet tooth.

Days in high school were made memorable for her because of Mrs. Alma Davis. She was a tall, slender lady with a neat hair cut who taught physical education. Marie remember her teaching various forms of dance. At Christmas Mrs. Davis put on an extravaganza. Students from each grade took part, and Mrs. Davis taught dances from the *Nutcracker Suite*. The dancers had fabulous attractive costumes. The audience sat in the bleachers of the gym. The music was loud, and the students all developed an appreciation for music and dance as a form of art. They all had a great sense of pride as they presented their new skills.

Some teachers just pop out in her mind when Mrs. Gee thinks back on those school days. Mr. Ben Holt, Ms. Grace Dupree, Mr. Neal Haywood, Mrs. Eva Champion, Mr. Roy Griffin, Ms. Jeanette Burroughs, and Mrs. Boulware all come to mind when she thinks of Hoffman Boston High School.

The basketball team was awesome. She remembers being one of the cheerleaders at Jenny Dean the year Hoffman Boston won the championship. She was wearing a blue felt skirt with a heavily starched crinoline slip under it to make it stand out. She jumped up and down so much when we won that she actually fainted.

She attended Virginia State College in Petersburg, Virginia. She was an elementary education major. She taught one and a half years in Arlington County, thirty-two years in the District of Columbia, and one year in Fairfax County. For the last thirteen years, she has been a substitute teacher.

In 1964 she married Mr. Lewis Gee. They are the proud parents of Gina Marie Roy and Judith Denise Gee-Wilson. They have nine grandchildren and one great grandchild.

Mrs. Gee spent her youthful days at Lomax with her best friend, Peggy Moore. Other close friends were Gary Boswell, Lolita Moore, and Audrey Payne. Today she sings in the gospel choir, Celestial Echoes. For about two years, God blessed her to participate in Total Praise. Total Praise was composed of four adults, almost senior women who did liturgical dancing. Her days spent expressing God's message, in physical motion, were the most thrilling events in her life. She treasures the days of her life spent in the Nauck Community (Source: Marie Gee)

Pamela Denise Preston

"Tuesday's Child is full of Grace"
Grace has many connotations that include effortless beauty and charm, refinement, generosity, and immunity. However, the definition of grace, which denotes my spirit, is protection given through God's favor.

Pamela Denise Preston is a living testament to God's favor. On a crisp, Tuesday morning on December 10 at 4:00 A.M., she was born to Loretta Preston at Columbia Hospital for Women in Washington, D.C. Although her earthly father did not embrace her, it was her Heavenly Father who saw fit to wrap her in His loving arms. She grew up in South Arlington in the Nauck community under the loving eyes of her grandmother, Lorraine Preston, and her mother. She was nurtured by the many saints who passed through the walls of Macedonia Baptist Church. Mrs. Funn read Bible stories that filled their tender ears with the love, forgiveness, and grace of God.

She recalls the gentle voice of Mrs. Yvonne Smith, who guided the young souls as she led the Bells of Joys in song to sing praises to God. They visited several churches in the Washington, D.C. area, allowing their little lights to shine as they represented Macedonia Baptist Church and the Nauck Community. She remembers faithfully attending Sunday school. In fact, it was there where Ms. Florence Terry, Mrs. Smith's aunt, nurtured her spirit to give her life to Christ. Mrs. Terry was the first to hug her intensely on that day.

The many families that comprised the Nauck community as she grew up offered her a sense of confidence, peace, pride, and support as she matriculated through the Arlington Public Schools. This community connection was paramount to her development because she would often be the only African American child in her class. Her mother would be the only African American parent at the PTA meetings or open house nights at school. Her community connection strengthened her commitment to excellence, while allowing her to connect with others who looked like her.

Mrs. Rena Taylor was her babysitter. She would go to her home after school each day when she attended Patrick Henry Elementary School. Mrs. Taylor taught her how to make pear preserve and homemade biscuits. She recalls many summers going out in Mrs. Taylor's backyard to the tree and picking cherries and pears. She would help Mrs. Taylor to wash clothes on a washing machine, where you had to manually put the garments through the rollers to wring out the water. Then they would put the washed clothes on the clothes line outback to dry. Mrs. Rena and her husband, Mr. Billy (William Taylor), brought Pamela her first African American Barbie. She stood three feet tall, and her hair rotated to change from black to brown. At this time, very few images of African American beauty were represented to African American girls in the media. By playing with this doll, she was able to develop a sense of pride and beauty. She remembers affirming her desire to become a model because she wanted to represent African American beauty in print. She still has the doll in her memorabilia chest.

Pamela played dolls with Ms. Roxie Green's great granddaughter, Sylvia Canada. April Powell and her mom, Mrs. Gladys, visited the neighbor who lived behind The Preston's, Mrs. Irene West. They would each hop the fence to play games together on Saturday or Sunday. Mrs. Irene's grandson, Cory, would often join them when he visited. Across the street lived Mr. and Mrs. Samuel Bellamy. Pamela grew up with their grandchildren, "Tidy," "Bookie," Lisa, Retta, and Joy. She had the biggest crush on Mr. and Mrs. Green's twin boys, David and Donald. They lived next door to Mr. and Mrs. Bellamy. She would watch them for hours throwing their football.

Her mom worked two jobs to buy her a moped one Christmas. She rode that scooter all over the Nauck community. She would zoom down to Kemper Road, where there was always something going on. Then she would go to Fort Bernard Park and fly down Walter Reed Drive to Nelson Street, down 22nd Street, and take Lincoln Street home. Wow! She had a ball growing up in the Nauck community. As time progressed, she carried all of these memories and more in her heart as she embarked on the next steps in her life. She sadly remembers the day she learned that Mrs. Rena passed away. This was her first encounter with death. She would walk by her house and long for her to come to the door.

Pamela graduated from Arlington Public Schools with honors and went on to graduate from Virginia Polytechnic Institute and State University in Blacksburg, Virginia, in 1990, earning a Bachelor's of Science in Urban Affairs and Planning with a minor in Political Science. In February 1991, God blessed her husband and her with their first child, Nandi Assata Alexander.

She recalled lamenting about how the neighborhood had changed. It did not look the same. This caused her a great deal of sadness because she knew she would never see or feel this close to any community or group of people again. Her daughter attended Abingdon Elementary, Gunston Middle School, and Wakefield High School. It was comforting to know that many community and church members were employed at her schools. They kept a watchful eye on her when she was at work. Pamela removed her for a short time to attend Maryland schools, but quickly brought her back to ensure she would have the nurturing she needed from her great-grandmother and church family.

Again God's favor touched her mind and her heart and led her to return to school after a seven-year break, earning her Master's in Education from George Washington University in Washington, D.C. in 1997. She received a second-grade teaching position at Edgar Allan Poe Elementary. In 1998 she was blessed with her second child, Jelan Halsten Preston-Boylan. While at Poe, she also taught fifth grade, served as technology and science coordinator and Title I resource teacher. She would later return to school, attending McDaniel College to receive her certification in administration before becoming an assistant principal at John H. Bayne Elementary School for six years. After completing the coursework for her doctoral studies in curriculum and instruction at the University of Phoenix, this Tuesday's child returned to the Suitland community to become principal of Suitland Elementary. Ironically, Suitland Elementary came to fruition after merging Edgar Allan Poe and Shadyside Elementary Schools in 2005.

Pamela would visit the Nauck community up until her aunt passed and she moved her grandmother and mother to live with them in their respective homes. They would continue going to the church. Pamela joined, First Baptist of Highland Park. After her grandmother died in 2011, it was difficult to return to the community. She did not know many of the faces. In fact, she could not speak the language of many of its inhabitants. Her grandmother loved to garden at her house at 2004 South Langley Street. Pamela did manage to retrieve the root of her favorite tree from the yard. She planted it in her yard, and it bloomed last year. The bloom reminded her of the joy she would experience each year as it bloomed on Langley Street.

Grace is the reoccurring theme of her life because like many young people, she stayed away from God, seeking happiness in all of the wrong places and faces. The prayers of her mother, aunt, and grandmother allowed her to remain on track for the purpose that God had for her life: the children. Her ministry is to serve the children by advocating for their right to a quality education in the classrooms of Prince George's County Public Schools.

While there are many days she felt that God had forsaken her, she is often reminded through the hugs, touches, smiles, and laughter of the children that her life is not in vain. She feels His power reverberating through her spirit, which serves to remind her that she has received His favor, and it is her responsibility to share it with others, especially the children, who too have His grace protecting their lives. They have the power to overcome their obstacles to make great things happen in their lives. Her journey back to the Suitland community has allowed her to see the awesome responsibility she has to assist families as they seek to navigate through life's challenges. However, none of this would be possible had it not been for her humble beginnings in the Nauck community, which provided her an understanding of two, very important lessons: one, it truly takes a village to raise a child; and two, God's favor over our lives has the power to guide and protect us as we fulfill His purpose for our lives. (Source: Pamela Preston)

Military

Lieutenant Leroy Taylor
Major General Robert C. Gaskill, Sr. (U.S. Army, Retired)
Flight Officer Nathaniel Rayburg
Major Gregory J. Wilson

Lieutenant Leroy Taylor

Leroy Taylor was born on April 15, 1910, in Washington, D.C., and was raised in Arlington, Virginia (Nauck), by his aunt and uncle, Nora and Overton Taylor, after the death of his father in a construction accident. He and his sister were raised with his cousins, Alfred, Ernest, William, Dorothy, and Verna, who were more like his brothers and sisters. He was educated in the public school system of Arlington, Virginia, and Washington, D.C. After graduation from college, he worked for the federal government in an administrative capacity until he was inducted into the Army at the age of thirty-two. He was inducted at Fort Myer, Virginia, on August 7, 1942. He was promoted to the rank of staff sergeant on June 5, 1943, with an M.O. of administrative clerk. He was discharged from the Army to accept an appointment without disruption to the Army Air Force's Officer's Candidate School in Miami Beach, Florida, where he graduated with the rank of second lieutenant. The Officer Candidate School began as a twelve-week course, but it expanded to sixteen weeks in 1943. Most of the Officer Training School (OTS) students were thirty years old or more, with the bulk of them in their thirties (Leroy was thirty-three years old) or forties. They came from all walks of life, but most were teachers, businessmen, or professionals. The majority were slated for administrative or instructional duties in the Air Force. After graduation he was stationed at Tuskegee Air Field as an administrative/personnel officer.

During his tenure on active duty, he was awarded a Good Conduct medal. He was discharged from the Air Forces Reserves on June 4, 1957, with the rank of first lieutenant. After his discharge, he returned to school to study law, which he practiced until his death on January 4, 1967. He was buried in Arlington Cemetery in Section 13, Site 16357 on January 9, 1967. (Source: Family history)

Major Robert C. Gaskill, Sr., (U.S. Army (Ret.)

Robert Gaskill entered the Army as a second lieutenant in 1952 with a bachelor's degree in business administration and a designation as a Distinguished Military Graduate from Howard University. He earned an M.B.A. at George Washington University, including the Army War College and the Executive Program in National and International Security University. He is also a graduate of several military schools and colleges at the John F. Kennedy School of Government at Harvard University.

General Gaskill's most recent command, before his retirement in 1981, was Deputy Commander of the Defense Logistics Agency in Alexandria, Virginia. General Gaskill's other commands include Deputy Commander at the Army War College in Carlisle Barracks, Pennsylvania; Deputy Commander of the 21st Support Command in Kaiserslautern, Germany; the First Support Brigade in Kaiserslautern; the Letterkenny Army Depot in Chambersburg, Pennsylvania; and the 5th Supply and Transport Battalion, 5th Infantry Division in Fort Carson, Colorado.

General Gaskill's contributions to the Quartermaster Corps are numerous. He personally directed the development of the Quartermaster-Commissary Procurement portion of the "Vietnamization Program" from 1969 to 1970. This ambitious program to make the Vietnamese people more self-sufficient included the aerial delivery of supplies to remote sites. As the first quartermaster to serve as the Deputy Commander of the Army War College, General Gaskill was able to shape logistical, financial, and personnel curriculum that affects today's senior Army leadership.

Gaskill retired from the Army after nearly twenty-nine years of service, in 1981. His honors include numerous U.S. and foreign decorations and awards. Among them are the U.S. Distinguished Service Medal, Legion of Merit, and several civilian and community service awards. He has been listed in *Who's Who in America* and was inducted into the Army Quartermaster Hall of Fame in 1994.

He taught business and public management at the Northern Virginia Community College for twenty years. He later served on the NVCC Board for three years. He is active in church and civic affairs. He also serves as an alumnus advisor to the ROTC cadets and cadre at Howard University. In 2011 Gaskill was honored by the Prince William Chapter of the NAACP with its Giving Back Award and the Washington Chapter of ROCKS, INC. presented him with its "1} (Source: Internet article).

Flight Officer Nathaniel Rayburg

Caption: Class 43-J graduated from flight training on Nov. 3, 1943, at Tuskegee Army Air Field in Alabama.
Order unknown: James B. Brown, Roger D. Brown, Herman R. Campbell Jr., Alfred Q. Carroll Jr., Clarence W. Dart, Charles W. Dickerson, Henri F. Fletcher, Perry E. Hudson Jr., Oscar D. Hutton, Haldane King, Edward Laird, Ivey L. Leftwich, Vincent J. Mason, Theodore H. Mills, Turner W. Payne, Gwynne W. Peirson, Harvey N. Pinkney, Nathaniel P. Rayburg, Emory L. Robbins Jr., Earl S. Sherrard Jr., Paul C. Simmons Jr., Eugene D. Smith, Jerome D. Spurlin, Nathaniel C. Stewart, Edward M. Thomas, William H. Thomas, William D. Tompkins, Hugh St. Clair Warner, and Leslie A. Williams; Album ID: 833672 Photo ID: 25502255

Nathaniel Rayburg graduated from flight training on November 3, 1943, at Tuskegee Army Air Field in Alabama. He was a member of Class 43-1. He was killed at Selfridge Field in Michigan on December 12, 1943, in a plane crash. He is buried in Section 8, Site 5470EH, at Arlington National Cemetery. (Source: Milton Rowe, Sr.)

Major Gregory J. Wilson

Gregory Wilson was the fifth child of Jerome Wilson and Idonia Wilson of Arlington, Virginia. He was born on June 27, 1956, at Freedmen's Hospital in Washington, D.C. (currently Howard University Medical Center). Greg attended Charles Drew Elementary School, Thomas Jefferson Middle School, Wakefield High School, and Virginia State University. While in college, he received a full, academic scholarship from the U.S. Army's ROTC Program. Greg received a B.A degree, cum laude, entered the Army as a second lieutenant, and retired as a major. While in the military, he served throughout the U.S. and in Korea and Germany.

Using the military's G.I. Bill, Greg attended Carnegie Mellon University, and in 1995, he received a Master's in Public Management. That same year, the U.S. Army featured Greg as their prototype for the Army's new Recruitment Program, a national advertising campaign with advertisements placed in *Ebony* Magazine, *Jet* Magazine and several Hispanic publications.

After completion of his master's degree, Greg went to work at the Cleveland Clinic Foundation, where he served as Corporate Manager for Diversity. He also served as Business Manager for the institution's Department of Gastroenterology, focusing on digestive diseases and prevention. He also worked for the City of Cleveland, Ohio, where he served as Secretary of the Civil Service Commission. While at the City of Cleveland, he also served as Assistant Commissioner for Water, where he managed the regional water distribution system and managed a workforce of 550 employees, including twenty-two labor unions.

Greg is currently Vice President and Georgia Area Manager for *CH2M HILL*, a global engineering firm with over thirty thousand employees. His responsibilities include oversight for the company's corporate affairs for the State of Georgia, including nine business units, over one thousand employees, and community involvement with elected officials throughout the State. He is active with several boards, chambers of commerce, and universities.

Greg and his wife, Pauline Malone-Wilson, have three children. They currently reside in Alpharetta, Georgia. (Source: Major Gregory J. Wilson)

Federal, State, and Local Government and Private Sector

Marcia Coachman Chapman
Naomi Yvonne Hawkins
Elmer L. H. Lowe, Sr.
William Augustus Rowe
Jaque' Tuck
Alfred O. Taylor, Sr.
Arlene Coachman Smith
Jacqueline Coachman
Tyrone E. Mitchell
Gerald Bullock

Marcia Coachman Chapman

Marcia Coachman Chapman, the youngest daughter of Ira W. and Audrey A. Coachman, and the sister of Jacqueline Coachman and Arlene Smith, was born in the District of Columbia at Freedmen's Hospital. She attended Drew Elementary/Model School and Stratford Junior High School, and she graduated from Woodlawn High School/Wakefield High School. She attended North Carolina Central University immediately after high school. However, later in life, she returned to college to graduate magna cum laude from Strayer University with a Bachelor of Business.

After working in the public works division of the Arlington County Government (following in the footsteps of her grandfather and many other family members), Marcia began a career with AT&T in 1990 as a temporary clerk, and is presently an operations analyst in the finance division. At AT&T she is an active member of the Women of AT&T and the Women of Finance. Her hobbies include gardening and genealogical research. She is blessed with two children, Andre and Vanessa, and a grandson, Skyler. (Source: Marcia Coachman Chapman)

Naomi Yvonne Hawkins

Naomi Yvonne Hawkins, a native of Washington, D.C., is the second of three children born to the late Thomas R. Gillis, Sr. and Naomi Katie Lansdowne Gillis. Her mother died when she was three years old, and her grandmother and stepmother, Carrie Paulding Gillis, helped to raise them. She attended kindergarten in D.C., Kemper/Drew Elementary in Arlington, Virginia, and Francis Junior High School and Dunbar Senior High School in D.C. She received her Bachelor of Arts from Howard University. She did graduate work at the Joint Military Intelligence College (JMIC).

Yvonne is retired from the National Security Agency (NSA) of Fort Meade, Maryland, where she worked for over thirty-four years as an analyst and ultimately chief. After her retirement, she started working for Hawkins Window Cleaning and Maintenance Company until 2002. She is an election officer for the Arlington County Electoral Board.

In the past, she has served on the Board of Directors of the Veterans Memorial YMCA and as an officer of the Jack & Jill Society of America. She also served on the PTAs of Drew, Our Savior Lutheran, Williamsburg, and Yorktown schools, and she was a member of the 19th Street Block Club of Nauck. For several years, she has done volunteer work with For Immediate Sympathetic Help (FISH) and voter registration. She is presently a member of the Phoenix Society, The Green Thumb Garden Club (both of NSA), and the JMIC Alumni Association.

Yvonne was baptized in the Macedonia Baptist Church at an early age, where she attended Sunday school and prayer meetings. She was also on the Junior Usher Board and junior choir. Presently she is a member of the Missionary Ministry, Gospel Chorus, and Unity in Worship. She served as the Vice Chairman of the Trustee Ministry.

Some of her hobbies include reading, puzzles, scrabble, gin rummy, and other board games. Her greatest gift is her love for God, her family, and church.

Yvonne was married to the late Leon Hawkins, and they have two sons, Derrick L. and Sean C., both of Arlington, Virginia. She is also the proud grandmother of two granddaughters and one grandson. (Source: Yvonne Hawkins)

Elmer L. H. Lowe, Sr.

Elmer L.H. Lowe, Sr. was born in Washington, D.C., and was raised in Arlington, Virginia. He attended Kemper and Drew Elementary Schools in Arlington and graduated from Hoffman Boston High school in Arlington. He is married to the former LaVonia Anthony. They have four adult children, Kim, Elmer Jr., Aja, and Ian.

After graduating from high school, he enlisted in the U.S. Air Force and remained there for twenty-four years, ten months and one day. He retired in the grade of master sergeant. During these years, he traveled to Germany, North Africa, France, England, and Alaska. However, he spent many years in the Washington area (at the Pentagon, at Arlington Hall Station, and at Bolling Air Force Base). While in the Air Force, he received many awards and decorations:

- Air Force Commendation Medal, 1968
- Joint Service Commendation Medal, 1972
- Air Force Commendation Medal (First Oak Leaf Cluster), 1976
- Meritorious Service Medal, 1977
- Meritorious Service Medal (First Oak Leaf Cluster), 1979
- Air Force Commendation Medal (Second Oak Leaf Cluster), 1981
- Many Air Force Good Conduct medals throughout his career

While in Alaska, he was also a candidate for the outstanding Airman in the Air Force. Upon retirement he was sworn in as a deputy sheriff in Arlington, Virginia. While working as a deputy sheriff, he attended Northern Virginia Community College and graduated with Associates in Applied Science, Administration of Justice. He holds active membership in many organizations:

- Life Member in the Air Force Sergeants Association
- Life Member in the National Assoc Of Blacks in Criminal Justice
- Life Member in the NAACP
- Member of American Legion Post 139; served as its post commander
- Over forty-four years as a member of Prince Hall Free Masons, Inc., jurisdiction of
- Virginia (Arlington Lodge #58); past master
- Over thirty-five years as a member of Prince Hall Shriner (AEAONMS), where he served as Illustrious Potentate in 1992 and received the Legion of Honor Certificate
- Received thirty-third and last degree in Masonry in 1990
- Received Department of Parks, Recreation, and Cultural Resources to honor Arlington's African-Americans who have demonstrated unsung leadership through their commitment to community, friends and family
- Member of the Macedonia Baptist Church for more than sixty-six years

Many County officials, church members, and Arlington residents have seen the results of his works in his present position as the president of the Arlington Branch of the NAACP. Under his leadership, they have been able to give over

$7,000 from the scholarship fund to Arlington County students who graduate from Arlington County High School. This year they will give over $30,000 in scholarships to deserving high school graduates. (Source: Elmer Lowe)

William Augustus Rowe

William August Rowe's accomplishments are well-documented in Arlington County, Virginia, publications. He served as a special policeman in 1869 and as Jefferson District Clerk of Elections and Collector in 1870. He was elected to the Jefferson District Board of Supervisors in 1871. He resigned that post in 1879 when he moved his family to Arlington County. That same year, he was elected to the Arlington Board of Supervisors and served until 1883. While serving on the Board, he became its first and only African American chairman. He was appointed Arlington County Superintendent of the Poor in 1883 and served until 1886. William was last listed on the 1900 U.S. Federal Census. The 1910 U.S. Federal Census listed Ellen, his wife, as a widow. Although the family continues to search for his date of death and burial place, the family estimates that he died around 1905.

According to the 1870 U.S. Federal Census, William was born in 1833. Oral history passed down through William's grandchildren told of his mother being a slave and his father a Stafford County plantation owner. William's father acknowledged him as a son and gave him the family name of Rowe.

He was taught to read and write (which was illegal during that time) and studied to be a blacksmith. At the start of the Civil War, he made war products for the Confederacy. When Union soldiers told William that he was a "fool" to make Confederate implements that would eventually be used to kill his own people, he left the plantation and followed the Union soldiers north. After the war, William returned to the plantation, picked up Ellen B., and migrated to Northern Virginia settling in Freedmen's Village.

William and Ellen married in 1867. They had nine children; however, only five survived beyond infancy. The children listed in the 1880 Census were George K., 6, 1867; Anne E., 6, 1869; John B., 6, 1871; Charles W., 6, 1876; and Robert C., 6, 1895. John lived to be twenty-four. Charles died at eight months of age, and Robert lived to be twenty-three.

George became a prominent realtor. He married Martha Ellen Burke and had eleven children. Anne taught school in Culpeper, Virginia, where she met and married Thomas West. They had eight children. Thomasyne West Gillis, the youngest, was William's last surviving grandchild. She died in 2005.

William and Ellen were among the founders of the Little Zion Church—known today as Lomax AME Zion Church—in Arlington, Virginia. They remained active members of the church throughout their lives.

Today there are more than 270 living descendants of William's sons, John and Robert D. Rowe. (Source: Milton Rowe, Sr.)

Comments:

The following resources were used for this article:

Oral history from Fannie Rowe Wair Smith, recorded by her granddaughter, Claudia Wair
Arlington Historical Magazine, Vols. 1, 2.2, and 3
Alexandria (Arlington) County, Virginia – 1853-1896 death records
Ancestry.com
United States Federal Census, 1990-1910
Arlington County Virginia – A History by C. B. Rose, Jr.

Jacque' Tuck

Do you have a desire to lend a helping hand in order to improve another person's life? Jaque' Tuck has identified this as her purpose in life. She spends time everyday helping others to overcome their problems and make their lives better.

Jaque' Tuck was born on February 11, 1984, in Arlington, Virginia. She was formally raised by her grandparents, Leroy and Queen Dunbar, in the Nauck "Green Valley" community. She, like many others in this community, was exposed to crime, gangs, violence, poverty, and drug activity. At an early age, Mrs. Tuck was grounded in the Christian faith. She became a member of the Macedonia Baptist Church, which was located in Arlington, Virginia. Her religious background set the foundation for her life and allowed her to escape the adversities that many of her family members and peers in her community faced.

Mrs. Tuck was educated in the Arlington Public Schools, where she received a high- quality education. She was educated at Drew Model, Gunston Middle, and Wakefield High School. She received an advanced diploma from Wakefield High School in 2002. Identifying with her passion to help others, Mrs. Tuck studied health science at George Mason University. In 2006 she received a Bachelor of Science degree. Midway through her studies at George Mason University, Mrs. Tuck recognized that her passion for people was greater than the health field and identified with the need to engage in integrative and holistic practices to help people make significant shifts in their lives. In 2007 she enrolled in the social work graduate program at Howard University and later received a Masters of Social Work degree in 2009.

Motivated to follow her passion, Mrs. Tuck obtained employment in 2004 at the Child and Family Services agency in Washington, D.C. She spent five years providing child welfare services to the District's children and families. Since 2009 Mrs. Tuck has been employed as a full-time Child Protective Services social worker for the Department of Human Services Agency, which is located in Arlington, Virginia. She is responsible for investigating allegations of abuse and neglect and providing supportive services to families. To that end, Ms. Tuck is also employed as a part-time, home-based counselor at Improving Outcomes, LLC, located in Falls Church, Virginia. She is responsible for providing crisis intervention and mental health services to at-risk children, youth, and their families.

On October 4, 2008, Mrs. Tuck married her high school sweetheart, Karl Tuck. They share one child, Kanoa Tuck, in common. Widely known for her "family first" motto, Mrs. Tuck exhibits a strong commitment to her family, which includes her extended relatives, and sets the foundation for a strong, fully functional family.

Despite experiences with various obstacles, Mrs. Tuck has stood committed to following her dreams. She puts all of her faith in God and uses Christian principles to guide her life. Her devotion to helping others has helped to improve the lives of individuals, families, and communities at large. Mrs. Tuck uses her experiences with obstacles as a self–motivator. She motivates others by helping them recognize that their differences make them beautiful and unique and their obstacles can be their paths to success. (Source: Jacque' Tuck)

Alfred O. Taylor, Sr.

Alfred O. Taylor, Sr., the oldest son of the late Overton and Nora Taylor, was born in Washington, D.C., on May 7, 1910, at their home at 347 22nd Street, N.W. His siblings were: Dorothy Hoffman, Verna Dean, Ernest, and William Taylor. He was brought to Arlington, Virginia, at a very early age and was educated in the Public School System of Arlington County (Kemper School) and in Washington, D.C., where he graduated from the Armstrong Technical High School in 1927. He was later employed by Arlington County in August 1928, where he retired as assistant superintendent in 1973, ending forty-four years of service.

During his forty-plus years of service, he was the recipient of many service awards, but the most cherished among them was when he and his two brothers, Ernest and William, were honored for a combined 110 years of service for Arlington County Government. It was made even more special because Ted Vactor of his favorite football team, the Washington Redskins, assisted in the presentation. On another occasion, he was cited in an article entitled, "Out with Flu, Arlington Aide Misses 40-Year Service Fete."

During a telephone interview, Taylor stated, "I've seen many changes here in Arlington. I remember when I first came to work in August 1928. There were no streets or avenues here. We went by so and so's farm for directions. Everything used to be referred to by farms.

"You know," Taylor continued, "I've never worked anywhere but here. I've been here so long, I wouldn't know anything else."

Taylor was known to assist people in the community to obtain employment with the County. It was often said, "If Mr. Taylor said you were okay, you were hired." Once he assisted a person in obtaining employment, he was known to not only mentor them, but would go to their homes to find out why they were not at work, often offering positive encouragement on why they should be there.

He was very active in his community and church. He was a member of the Macedonia Baptist Church and joined in 1926. He was a member of the first choir, which was organized in 1927. He also served as the sexton, church treasurer, and member of the trustee board. He was also active in the Nauck Citizens Association, the NAACP, and he was a charter member of the Y's Men's Service Club of the Veterans Memorial YMCA. During World War II, he served as one of the air raid wardens for the Nauck community.

Married to the late Ruby Leona Gaines, they were privileged to celebrate fifty years of happiness in 1979. To their union were two children, Audrey Coachman and Alfred, Jr. Mr. Taylor passed on December 2, 1985. (Source: Oral history and past articles from family)

Arlene Coachman Smith

Arlene Coachman Smith was born to the union of the late Audrey A. and Ira W. Coachman in August of 1951. Arlene attended Arlington County public schools (Drew Elementary, Kemper School, Thomas Jefferson, and Hoffman-Boston). Arlene worked at Defense Communications Agency (DCA), part-time, and graduated from Wakefield High School in 1969. She attended Virginia State College, and during the summer months, she obtained temporary jobs. She was unexpectedly offered a full-time, permanent position at Raby & Stafford Law Offices and did not return to college.

She gained first-hand experience and was able to take that experience to apply and get several jobs during her early years. After being in an office, she decided she wanted to work outdoors, so she applied for a position as a Metro bus driver. She loved working outdoors and with the public but, after nine years at Metro, she decided it was time to go back into the office. Through temporary agencies, Arlene again secured a permanent position at the American Society of Travel Agents, a travel association headquartered in Alexandria, Virginia. She began her career there as a secretary to one of the directors and, after a few years, was promoted to executive assistant to the director of the Association. This position afforded Arlene the opportunity to travel extensively to both domestic and international destinations, such as Morocco, Europe, Yugoslavia, Ireland, Hong Kong, Taiwan, and many other exciting venues. She worked for ASTA for sixteen years. Due to deregulation and other cutbacks in the travel industry, the agency no longer received dues from travel agents, which meant ASTA had to lay off employees, and Arlene was one of them. After re-accessing her options, she decided to go into the government. Again she got her foot in the door through a temporary agency and landed a position at the United States Mint.

Arlene first worked in the sales and marketing department as a program assistant. She worked on the Atlantic Olympic Task Force, promoting the Olympic Coin. A few years later, she was promoted to the Office of Management Services as a support services specialist. She was in charge of ensuring that all services within the building were met (e.g., conference room schedules, fleet, the Public Transportation Incentive Program, and five, mentally challenged mailroom employees from whom she learned so much about being thankful).

Arlene went back to college and received her Bachelor of Science in Business Administration from the University of the District of Columbia. Fifteen-plus years later, she is currently the property/fleet manager at Headquarters in Washington, D.C., where she is responsible for the tracking and accountability of United States Mint property (e.g., CPUs, monitors, laptops, and Blackberries).

As property/fleet manager, Arlene responds to quarterly data calls from the Department of Treasury and General Services Administration (GSA). She furnishes data, such as vehicle inventory, Greenhouse Gas (GHG) usage, and mileage information on thirty-one United States Mint vehicles. She oversees five other field sites: United States Bullion Depository (USBD Fort Knox, Kentucky); West Point, New York; Denver, Colorado; San Francisco, California; and Philadelphia, Pennsylvania to ensure their property and fleet are in compliance.

Arlene is married to Kent W. Smith. They have two daughters, two granddaughters, and one grandson. Her favorite pastimes include gardening, yard sales and, most especially, spending time with family. (Source: Arlene Coachman Smith)

Jacqueline Coachman

Jacqueline Coachman was a student at Wakefield High School in Arlington, Virginia, at the time the nation struggled with the Vietnam War, the Civil Rights movement, and urban violence. The loss of American soldiers as well as the suffering of Vietnamese civilians impacted her view of the world. The Civil Rights movement shed light on the discrepancy between American ideals and the realities of being an American of color, resulting in her deep passion for truth and integrity. And urban violence of the 1960s and 70s evoked a lasting commitment to making life better in urban neighborhoods. It was these priorities that guided Jacqueline's academic training at Syracuse University.

The focus of a Bachelor's in Economics/Sociology at Syracuse and a Master's in Public Administration from the esteemed Maxwell School of Syracuse was acquiring the expertise to devise, implement, and evaluate urban quality of life initiatives. The federal government was making huge investments in reducing urban poverty and blight. It was the conviction of Jacqueline that if these initiatives were to truly bring about a new day, there must be accountability for results—or lack thereof. To that end, she took courses in quantitative analysis, research, budgeting, and local government management and policy. She earned both a bachelor and master in four years—and did so with honors.

Jacqueline left Syracuse with a burning passion to bring her talents to bear in distressed, urban neighborhoods. Her first job was Assistant to the Mayor of Newark, New Jersey. At Howard University, she managed the Master's in Urban Studies program, as well as an initiative by three universities in support of the Adams Morgan Organization (the premiere community-based organization in a neighborhood in the early stages of re-gentrification). Other service includes Assistant to the Executive Director of the Housing Opportunities Commission of Montgomery County, Maryland; Assistant to the Executive Director of the Maryland-National Capital Park & Planning Commission; and Planning Board Administrator for Prince George's County, Maryland.

In 1990 Jacqueline pursued her dream of providing consulting services to neighborhood revitalization initiatives. She served as a consultant to revitalization projects of Prince George's County; the City of Mount Rainier, Maryland; and the Town of Fairmount Heights, Maryland, as well as the St. Paul Community Development Corporation, the Congress of National Black Churches, Public Technology, Inc. (an affiliate of the International City Managers Association), and a task force convened by Nations Bank. She was later blessed with the opportunity to serve the Nauck community, where she was raised and continues to reside. Jacqueline provided research, statistical, and grant-writing support to the revitalization agenda launched by the Bonder and Amanda Johnson Community Development Corporation.

While working as an independent consultant, Jacqueline also served as a substitute teacher in the middle schools of Alexandria, Virginia. It was this experience that revealed her God-given purpose: to protect the children. She transitioned from protecting urban neighborhoods to protecting the children that call those neighborhoods home. Jacqueline currently serves as Youth Services Program Specialist for the City of Alexandria. Her accomplishments include a wealth of activities to impress upon teens the importance of abstinence/safe sex; providing leadership to the development of a youth master plan; and publishing an online newsletter on youth well-being.

Jacqueline's entire life has been governed by the belief that one person can make a difference. She has walked that walk regardless of the personal consequences. Her motto is, "If not you, then who?" (Source: Jacqueline Coachman)

Tyrone Edwin Mitchell, Sr.

Tyrone Edwin Mitchell, Sr. was born on February 6, 1971, in the Nauck community; the same proud, African American Community where his father, Calvin Mitchell, and his paternal grandparents, Alzenia Coachman Mitchell and Arnett Mitchell, lived for over fifty years. His mother, Lueida Bolden Mitchell, was born in Meridian, Mississippi, the daughter of Queen Esther and Jesse Bolden.

Tyrone attended Claremont Elementary School, Kenmore Intermediate School, and graduated with honors from Yorktown High School. While at Yorktown, he participated in several extra-curricular activities and excelled in football and wrestling. He won the District championship in wrestling during his junior year. Tyrone says a defining moment in his life occurred when his guidance counselor called him to her office, sat him down, and told him that he had an important decision to make: *What was he going to do with his life?* To help him with his decision making, she showed him the salaries for engineers and other professions. She then asked if he wanted the ability to provide lucratively for his future family. She challenged him to choose, right then and right there, if he wanted just a job or a promising career after he completed his education. The choice was his to make. Tyrone decided he wanted a career and, with the help of this dedicated counselor, his supportive family, a caring faculty, and his entire "village," Tyrone began to seriously prepare for his future.

Tyrone attended Howard University in Washington, D.C. and graduated from the College of Engineering with a Bachelor of Science in Mechanical Engineering in December 1994. While at Howard, he participated in the American Society of Mechanical Engineers and the National Society of Black Engineers, and he became an active member of the Kappa Alpha Psi Fraternity. He also served as an intern at General Electric and the Amoco Oil Company while he was a student at Howard. Although he has traveled, worked, and lived in several states across the country, Tyrone has maintained a close relationship with his community, high school, and college friends.

Tyrone has worked in the oil and gas industry since his graduation from Howard University. He has held a number of progressively more challenging positions and has been promoted and relocated several times. He began his career as a project engineer with Amoco Oil in January 1995 at the Whiting Refinery in Whiting, Indiana. He held several engineering positions at several sites until he was promoted to engineering manager at BP's Texas City Refinery. Tyrone then served in several operations management roles, where he managed manufacturing teams.

In July 2007, he was promoted to business performance manager at the BP Texas City Chemical Plant. There he was responsible for managing the site's $80 million budget and negotiating land leases and commercial agreements. He was credited with turning around the financial performance of the site by creating efficiencies and processes that reduced costs by $7 million without affecting the safety of the plant.

In July 2009, Tyrone was promoted to regional operations manager and relocated to Atlanta, Georgia. In this position, his responsibilities included providing overall leadership and assurance in managing the operations for BP pipelines and terminals located east of the Rocky Mountains. Five district managers report directly to Tyrone, and he is held accountable for an asset base that includes eight gas and oil pipeline systems and twenty-five gas loading terminals. The region has approximately three hundred employees.

Tyrone also serves as the president of Olympic Pipe Line Company, which is located in Seattle, Washington. The position also holds accountability for BP's Northwest gas terminals.

Tyrone and his wife, Alexis, are the proud parents of three children, Tyler, Tyrone, Jr. (TJ), and Alexia. (Source: Tyrone E. Mitchell)

Gerald Bullock

Gerald Bullock was born in Arlington, Virginia, in 1936. He is the son of the late George W. Bullock, Jr. and Christine Bullock. He is the brother of Willie Bullock and a twin sister, Geraldine Bullock, M.D. He attended Stevens Elementary and Francis Junior High Schools in Washington, D.C., and graduated from Hoffman-Boston High School. He attended Virginia State College, and in 1956, he began his storied and illustrious career with the United States Government. He is a member of Lomax A.M.E. Zion Church.

Gerald, a member of Defense and Maritime Operations Division's (DMO) Advanced Marine Center (AMC) Business Area and was selected as the winner of CSC's North American Public Sector (NPS) 2009 Presidential Award for Career Achievement.

Gerald has over fifty years of experience as a Navy food service facilities specialist. He has extensive expertise in matters dealing with food service systems concepts, the design and arrangement of general mess equipment, and the development of feeding proficiency and training modules. Gerald's work includes underway inspections and modernizations of food service facilities for existing ships, and the conceptual design, detail design, and acceptance testing of food service facilities for new construction and conceptual ships. He played a major role in the design of food service facilities for a wide variety of U.S. Navy surface ships, including the CVN 68 Class and the new CVN 78 Class aircraft carriers, CG 47 Class cruisers, DDG 963 and DDG 51 Class destroyers, and FFG7 Class frigates. Gerald also developed food service system concepts for a variety of new ship concepts, including the LHAR, MPF, LMSR, MLP, and JHSV ships.

Additionally, Gerald developed and implemented an innovative centralized galley concept for the LSD 41 Class ships. He has also supported the design of numerous Navy shore-side food service facilities at the request of the Naval Facilities Engineering Command, and his most famous design to date is the Navy mess kitchen in the West Wing of the White House. He was also instrumental in designing a kitchen at Fort David. Gerald is recognized by his customers and his peers alike as the nation's single, top expert in naval ship food service systems. He has taken the initiative to maintain his status as the U.S. Navy's foremost subject matter expert in the area of food service, serving the repository for critical Naval Ship Food Service System new design, inspection, and system upgrading skills. If it were not for Gerald, the U.S. Navy would have lost their corporate history in the food service area several years ago, and would no longer have these skills and capabilities available for both the design of new ships, and for updating and modernizing the food service systems on existing ships.

Gerald has received numerous letters of appreciation, outstanding and superior performance citations, and meritorious service awards. Gerald's current aircraft carrier customers refers to him as a "National Treasure," stating that there is no one else available in the country, either within or outside of the U.S. Navy that remotely approaches Gerald's level of knowledge and capability. This customer states simply that when Gerald is involved, the job is done right, and with full consideration of the impact of food service system design on the real integrated design of the ship.

Gerald's professionalism, technical expertise, and dedication demonstrate the best of CSC's values. When a food service issue arises for a U.S. Navy or military sealift command ship, the ship design manager is directed to talk to Gerald Bullock at CSC for identifying the best solution to the problem. Gerald has earned the complete trust, confidence, and respect of his customers, colleagues, and peers. He derives great personal satisfaction from his work and is totally dedicated to doing the right thing for the Sailor. It is an honor to have Gerald on the CSC DMO Team. (Source: Copied from DMO document)

Religion

Dr. Leonard L. Hamlin Sr.
Dr. Leonard N. Smith
Reverend Richard O. Green, Sr.
Reverend Augustus Henderson
Reverend Evelyn Henderson King
Reverend Ely Williams, Jr.
Minister-in-Training Noreen Murphy Freeman
Minister Janice Preston-Clarke
Minister Tonia Heggs
Minister Dejohn Campbell
Reverend Morris Gregory Williams
Minister-in-Training Cheryl Henderson
Reverend Ernie Moore

Dr. Leonard L. Hamlin, Sr.

Dr. Leonard L. Hamlin, Sr., currently serves as the pastor of the Macedonia Baptist Church in Arlington, Virginia. Since coming to Macedonia in July 1996, the fellowship has strengthened numerically and spiritually. The ministry has grown from one to two Sunday worship services, and a noon, day worship has been instituted, which is held monthly. Numerous ministries, discipleship classes, and mission efforts have been organized and are operating to meet the needs of the congregants and the community. Due to a concern for community, the Bonder and Amanda Johnson Community Development Corporation was founded in 1999. Design was completed and financing secured for the construction of a thirty-six-unit, affordable housing, mixed-use, development project. The Macedonian Housing Project was completed and opened for occupancy in May 2011. The development includes ground floor space for the church business offices and the Nauck Community Services Center. The Macedonian Housing Project has received LEED certification as the most energy-efficient, multi-family unit in Northern Virginia. In 2007 the purchase of the former Arlington Veteran's Memorial YMCA was completed, and the facility was transformed into the Macedonia Baptist Church Family Life Center. The property consists of an administration building and outdoor pool. Prayers and plans are in process for the improvement and development of the Family Life Center in an effort to better serve the Macedonia Baptist Church Ministry and the community. In addition to the properties listed, the church has purchased additional land of which one of the four sites is currently being used for a community business.

Dr. Hamlin received a Bachelor of Business Administration degree (1983) from the Howard University School of Business; a Master of Divinity degree (1984); and a Doctor of Ministry degree from the Howard University School of Divinity (1996). He has served as a Ford Foundation research fellow and was the recipient of the Benjamin E. Mays Scholarship for Education and Commitment to the ministry. Dr. Hamlin completed the Summer Leadership Continuing Education Program (SLI) of the Harvard Divinity School in Cambridge, Massachusetts, in April 2005. The executive training program is for clergy, lay leaders, and community activists who are involved in faith-based community and economic development. Dr. Hamlin is also a graduate of Leadership Arlington, class of 2001, and a recipient of Leadership Arlington's Leadership Legacy Award. Dr. also serves as a chaplain to the Arlington County Fire Department.

Dr. Hamlin is married to Machell Nicholson Hamlin, Esq., and is the proud father of one son, Leonard L. Hamlin, Jr., a 2006 honors graduate of DeMatha Catholic High School, in Hyattsville, Maryland, and a 2010 graduate of Saint John's University in Queens, New York, where he majored in business management. (Source: Excerpted from web page)

Dr. Leonard N. Smith

Dr. Leonard N. Smith proudly serves as the Senior Minister of Mount Zion Baptist Church, Arlington, Virginia. His unique, uncompromising, and bold approach to presenting God's Word is renowned for reforming lives and advancing God's Kingdom.

Through the dedicated headship of Dr. Smith, Mount Zion is flourishing delightfully as a "Kingdom Focused" church. Since his arrival in 1991, the membership has grown significantly. His eagle-like vision has resulted in the establishment of a burgeoning spirit of ministry, which consists of five, core ministries: Outreach, Family Life, Christian Educational, and Creative Arts and Foundational ministries. Birthed from those main ministries are twenty-two sub-ministries that are comprised of forty committees.

Via programs that provide tutoring, food assistance, and financial support, the spirit of the "Church on the Hill" has extended to local community residents and agencies, as well as people organizations, state and nationwide. Mount Zion's Radio Outreach Ministry has also supplied a bountiful blessing to the Washington Metropolitan region. Dr. Smith can be heard on WYCB – 1340 AM every Saturday at 4:30 P.M. and Monday at 6:00 P.M. On Sundays at 6:30 A.M., his moving messages are aired on New Inspirational Praise 104.1 FM. Dr. Smith is seen live, via the Internet, every Sunday morning at 9:30 A.M. on Baptist Television Network (www.baptisttelevision.com).

In May 2009, Dr. Smith was installed as the President of the Virginia Baptist State Convention, Virginia's oldest African American convention of Baptist churches. He serves as a Chaplain for both Arlington County Fire and Police Departments and is the C.E.O. of Leonard N. Smith Ministries.

Born in Baltimore, Maryland and partly raised in the District of Columbia, Dr. Smith's walk with God was fueled by the loving tutelage of his grandmother. It's become familiar practice to honor his grandmother's discipleship by infusing stories of her Christian teachings into his powerful sermons. Lessons learned inside the boundaries of grandma's house have matured into a ministry preached on four continents. His twenty-five years of pastoral excellence began in 1985 when the Union Baptist Church (Gordonsville, Virginia) inaugurated him as their pastor. Four years later, he was chosen to shepherd Rivermont Baptist Church (Lynchburg, Virginia). Mount Zion tabbed the budding author in 1992 to become Dr. Oswald C. Smith's (the two pastors are not related) successor.

Equipped with a Master of Divinity, a Doctorate of Ministry, and eight honorary degrees, Dr. Smith is continually pursuing opportunities to further his education. He is the immediate past president of Richmond Virginia Seminary, in Richmond, Virginia; a doctoral mentor at United Theological Seminary in Dayton, Ohio; a lecturer in the National Congress of Christian Education; and is a co-chair for the Minister's Division of the Progressive National Baptist Convention. Among Dr. Smith's many professional achievements, nothing renders him prouder than his personal achievement of being the loving father of his children, Tiffany and Phillip.

Reverend Richard O. Green, Sr.

Reverend Richard O. Green, Sr. is a native Arlingtonian. He is the son of the late Lillian and Richard Green. He is the oldest of four children (two sisters and one brother). He is married to the former Betty Briggs of Washington, D.C., and the father of two sons: Richard Jr., and Stefan. He is an associate minister of the Mount Zion Baptist Church in Arlington, Virginia.

Reverend Green was educated in the schools of Northern Virginia and the District of Columbia and furthered his education in a field of value to others by attending college. His vocation in life has certainly reflected the desire to be of service to mankind. He has served two school systems (Northern Virginia and the District of Columbia) as an automotive instructor.

Reverend Green's vocation choice of automotive mechanics was not offered in his all-black high school, Hoffman-Boston. After much pressure from his parents and the NAACP, in 1949 he was sent to Manassas Regional High School. With the continuation of a court fight, in 1950 he entered the all-white Washington-Lee High School to further his studies. Still continuing his education, he attended St. Paul Polytechnic Institute in Lawrenceville, Virginia, and Howard University in Washington, D.C. He was later hired by the District of Columbia as an automotive instructor. While there he was offered and accepted the position of automotive instructor at Washington-Lee High School in Arlington, Virginia.

A few of his present and past community affiliations include: member, Nauck Revitalization Organization (NRO); member, Nauck Civic Association and NAACP; member, Intensive Drug Treatment Component Advisory Committee; member, Drew School Advisory Committee; member, Substance Abuse Advisory Board, Arlington, Virginia; board member, American Red Cross, Arlington Chapter; member, Northern Virginia Baptist Ministers Conference; co-Chairman and organizer, Parent-Family Support Group, Arlington, Virginia; co-organizer, Green Valley Crack Down on Drugs Patrol; volunteer, Arlington County Detention Facility; member of the board of directors of the YMCA-Veterans Memorial Branch and Arlington United Way Executive Committee; and numerous awards, too many to mention at this time.

His past business ventures include owning a Texaco Station in Washington, D.C; opening the first African American used auto sales and service in South Arlington; and opening an auto sales service in Smithfield, North Carolina.

Reverend Green is a man of God who walks the life he speaks about every day. He has certainly been instrumental in the life of churches of the community, collectively and individually. He is grateful to have served the Mount Salvation Baptist Church as Assistant to the Pastor for many years and one year as Interim Pastor. The community certainly has been stabilized by his many, untiring efforts. We must not forget the many youth who have been guided by his direction and advice to lead lives, which have led to higher stages of production. Only a man who has the living God in his life can display morality of such high and distinguishing qualities. (Source: Reverend Richard O. Green, Sr.)

Reverend Augustus Henderson

Reverend Augustus Henderson has served as pastor of the Christian Way Baptist Church in Falls Church, Virginia, since September 1995.

A native of Arlington, Virginia (Green Valley), his wife, Jacqueline, their three children, Joshua Augustus, Aaron Timothy, and Jordan Matthew Peele, currently reside in Fort Washington, Maryland. Pastor Henderson is a graduate of Wilbur H. Waters School of Religion and Theological Seminary in Washington, D.C., where he is a former instructor; he received his Master of Theological Degree in May 2011. In October 2011, he received an award from the school for distinguishing himself in the faith community and reflecting positively upon the school. He serves as a member of the Board of Directors.

He was licensed to preach the Gospel in June 1980 under the leadership of Dr. Carroll Baltimore, former pastor, Mount Pleasant Baptist Church, and was ordained to assist Pastor Harry J. Pilson, current pastor, of the Mount Pleasant Baptist Church in June 1994.

Pastor Henderson has allowed the Holy Spirit to guide him as pastor of Christian Way Baptist Church. Under his pastorate, Christian Way Baptist Church has changed all departments, boards, and auxiliaries to ministries with the focus on service. The following ministries were formed: Marriage and Family Enrichment, Christian Counseling, Women's Ministry, Men's Ministry, Singles Ministry, Prison Ministry, and the Youth Ministry. The Christian Way website has also been formed.

Pastor Henderson is serving as third-vice moderator for the Northern Virginia Baptist Association. He served as president of the Baptist Ministers Conference of Northern Virginia and Vicinity from September 2006 to July 2008. He served two terms as first vice president and one term as second vice president. Pastor Henderson served as secretary and financial secretary of the Baptist Ministers Conference of the City of Alexandria and vicinity. He has been appointed to the Ordination Council and elected to the Executive Board for the Northern Virginia Baptist Association. He has been appointed to the Executive Board of the Baptist Ministers Conference of Northern Virginia and Vicinity for two presidents.

Pastor Henderson has a burden for young people. He coached youth basketball for more than ten years and baseball for three years. He was involved in many activities at Oxon Hill High School and Oxon Hill Middle School, where he received the Volunteer of the Year Award, serving as the mentor coordinator and boys' basketball coach. At Oxon Hill High School, he held memberships in several groups and served as president of the Oxon Hill High School Boys Basketball Parent Support group for three years. (Source: Reverend Augustus Henderson)

Reverend Evelyn Henderson King

Reverend Evelyn King was licensed and ordained as a minister of the Gospel at Macedonia Baptist Church, Arlington, Virginia, under the pastorate of Reverend Dr. Leonard L. Hamlin, Sr. In her many leadership capacities at Macedonia, she served as Director of Support Ministries, Missions and Outreach, Youth Ministries, Vacation Bible School, tribe coordinator of South Arlington membership, and wedding coordinator. Ever the servant, she served in more than one position at a time. Her favorite ministry was Congregational Care. Though the ministry was birthed in Reverend King, Pastor Hamlin embraced it as an opportunity to meet the needs of the congregation.

Reverend King's passions include proclaiming the Gospel of Jesus Christ to all who will listen, and bringing private worship to the sick and shut in. Reverend King is the Visionary and Founder of You 'Can' Get Up Now Ministries, which seeks to live the mandate of the Great Commission, Matthew 28:18-20.

After serving as Interim Pastor at the Laurel Grove Baptist Church for two and half years, God assigned Reverend King to serve as the Servant Pastor of the Greater Gospel Church, a new mission ministry, whose mission is, *Living the Great Commission*, with a vision that is committed to God, connected to Christ, communicating His love, and consistent in His service. In Pastor King's words: "At GGC we are putting action behind the WORD of God by taking the message and ministry from the seat to the street."

Under the leadership of Pastor King, Greater Gospel is holding true to its mission. The church has engaged in helping homeless children, providing shoes for Haiti, ministering to Manor Care Nursing Home, and supporting the U.S. Army troops via a financial workshop for living successfully. GGC received the Volunteer of the Year Award, 2012 for its exemplary outreach to the Manor Care health facility. To God be the Glory!

Reverend King graduated from Wakefield High School in Arlington County and the John Leland Center for Ministerial Studies; was certified at Gordon-Conwell Theological Seminary/Preaching College; and studied at Averett University, Strayer University, and the Virginia Theological Seminary

Reverend King is married to Deacon Albert King. She is the mother of four children, two foster children, and the proud grandmother of eight.

Reverend King's personal motto is: *"Saved and sent to serve; committed to consistently communicating the love of Christ in every situation and circumstance in order that all may know they are forever connected to God; putting action behind the WORD of God; and taking the Gospel message and ministry from the seat to the street."* (Source: Reverend Evelyn King)

Reverend Ely Williams, Jr.

Reverend Ely Williams, Jr. was born September 6, 1931. He is the youngest of five children to the late Ely Williams, Sr. and Isnora Ivey Williams in Roanoke Rapids, North Carolina. He was educated in the public schools of Roanoke Rapids, North Carolina, the District of Columbia, and the Arlington County Public Schools, where he graduated from Hoffman Boston High School in January 1950. He received his formal education from the Manhattan Technical Institute in New York City; the Newark College of Engineering in Newark, New Jersey; and the Washington Baptist Seminary in Washington, D.C. For forty years, Reverend Williams served as a general contractor and the owner/operator of Network Sedan, a limousine service, until his retirement.

Reverend Williams accepted Christ at an early age and cast his lot with the Macedonia Baptist Church of Arlington, Virginia, under the pastorate of the late Reverend Sherman W. Phillips. During his residency in Newark, New Jersey, Reverend Williams joined the Greater Harvest Baptist Church under the pastorate of the Reverend Charles Banks. Upon his return to Arlington, Virginia, Reverend Williams reunited with the Macedonia Baptist Church under the pastorate of the late Reverend Dr. Clarence A. Robinson, Sr. As a faithful and obedient servant of God, he yielded to the Call and was licensed and ordained to the Gospel Ministry.

Upon the retirement of Dr. Clarence A. Robinson, Reverend Williams served faithfully and dutifully as co-interim pastor with the Reverend Clemmie R. Griffin, until the Pulpit Search Committee, of which he was a member, extended the Call to Pastor to Reverend Dr. Leonard L. Hamlin, Sr. In October 2000, Reverend Ely Williams united with the Sanctuary at Kingdom Square (formerly known as Gelndale Baptist Church) under the pastorate of Reverend Anthony G. Maclin. Reverend Williams served as Minister to the Seniors and Charge Minister for Fifth Sundays. He also served with the Married Couples Sunday School Class. He was a thirty-second-degree Mason, a Past Master and member of Arlington Lodge #58, Shadrack Jackson Consistory, and Galconda Temple #24 A.E.A.O.N.M.

On Tuesday morning, July 26, 2005, Reverend Ely Williams, Jr. completed his earthly work and stepped onto the streets of glory and was received into the arms of Jesus. (Source: Obituary program)

Minister-in-Training Noreen Freeman Murphy

M.I.T. Noreen Murphy, a native of Arlington, Virginia, was adopted by the late Deacon Henry and Verna Taylor-Dean of Arlington, Virginia. Noreen joined the Macedonia Baptist Church and started singing at the early age of eight in the Bells of Joy Children's Choir, under the direction of Kenny Taylor. Noreen is married to Staff Sergeant Ronald C. Murphy, and they have two children: LaShawna Renee' Freeman and Ronald Cordell Murphy Jr.

Noreen accepted her call into ministry in 2006, when she began preparation because she realized ministry required continuous preparation, prayer, commitment, and a sincere love for God and God's people. God allowed Noreen the opportunity to travel to Paris, France, to record as a vocalist for Liz Macomb, a well- known jazz gospel artist. Noreen has recorded solo and back-up for Country Gospel Artist Alexandria Lajoix. In Addition, God has afforded Noreen many opportunities to sing back-up for other artists, such as Monique Walker, Angela Spivey, and a host of local and national artists, including Pastor Tyrone Jefferson, which led to an appearance on the *Bobby Jones Gospel Show*.

Noreen has served in various ministries at Macedonia Baptist Church. Noreen received a Bachelor of Science in Computer Networking, with a minor in Business Management from Strayer University, and her Master of Divinity degree from Howard University School of Divinity. Noreen is now pursuing her Doctorate of Education in Pastoral and Community Counseling at Argosy University. Presently Noreen is serving in the Minister in Training Program and the Evangelism and Global Missions Ministry. Noreen's favorite scripture can be found in Proverbs 3:5-6: "Trust in the Lord with all your heart and lean not unto your own understanding, in all your ways acknowledge Him and He will strengthen your heart." Noreen loves the Lord God with all her heart, mind, soul, and strength, and her prayer is that she will lead a life that will always exalt God that He will draw others to Him. (Source: Minister Noreen Freeman Murphy)

Minister Janice Preston-Clarke

Minister Janice Preston-Clarke has been a member of Macedonia Baptist Church since early childhood, dedicating her life to Christ at the age of eleven. Janice has worked faithfully in the ministry for several years, and her enthusiasm and excitement about the Kingdom of God is evident to all she comes in contact with, whether in the work-place, on the prayer line, or in the church. She has devoted her life to serving others through various charities, such as Martha's Table/McKenna's Wagon; D.C. Central Kitchen; and a number of non-profit organizations, including Granville Academy, the American Red Cross, the Lupus Foundation of America, and the Alzheimer's Association. With the joy of the Lord as her strength, Janice is currently focused on the start-up, Extend Your Love Foundation, along with her daughter, Anneka, with the goal of the foundation being to extend love to women and their families that are affected by cancer.

2 Corinthians 12:9-10 (NASB): "And He has said to me, 'My grace is sufficient for you, for power is perfected in weak-ness.' Most gladly, therefore, I will rather boast about my weaknesses, so that the power of Christ may dwell in me. Therefore I am well content with weaknesses, with insults, with distresses, with persecutions, with difficulties, for Christ's sake; for when I am weak, then I am strong." This verse led Janice to accept the call that God has on her life. Janice was licensed to preach the Gospel on May 30, 2012, by Reverend Dr. Leonard L. Hamlin, Sr. of Macedonia Baptist Church in Arlington, Virginia. Janice currently serves as Director of Cornerstone Life Ministries at Macedonia Baptist Church, which encompasses the Women, Men, Young Adults, Employment, Forerunners, Couples, Family Life, and Recreation Ministries. Janice also leads the Early Rise Prayer Line and has facilitated workshops, led Bible studies, and continues to seek God first in all that she does.

Although Janice was born in Tuskegee, Alabama, she grew up from the age of two in Arlington, Virginia, and is a graduate of the Arlington County Public School System. She considers Arlington her home. Janice attended Trinity College in Washington, D.C., and completed her biblical studies at the Washington Bible College and Capital Bible Seminary in Lanham, Maryland. She now resides in Clinton, Maryland, with her husband, Dean, and she is currently em-ployed by the Public Affairs Support Services, Inc. as a compliance manager, monitoring campaign finance. (Source: Minister Janice Preston-Clarke)

Minister Tonia Heggs

Minister Tonia Heggs' foundation of living is found in Matthew 6:33: "Seek ye first the kingdom of God and all his righteousness, and all these things shall be added unto you."

Tonia began her progressive walk of belief, faith, and trust in God at the St. John Baptist Church in Alexandria, Virginia, under the pastorate of Reverend Dr. John W. Johnson for thirty-four years, during which she served in numerous capacities of ministry leadership.

Under the unction and direction of the Holy Spirit, Tonia united with Macedonia Baptist Church on Sunday, May 16, 2004, under the pastorate of Reverend Dr. Leonard L. Hamlin, Sr., where she served as a prayer ministry leader, deaconess, and minister-in-training. On Wednesday, May 30, 2012, Tonia was licensed to preach the Gospel of Jesus Christ by Reverend Hamlin and now serves as Director of Christian Education over the following ministries: Discipleship Sunday School; Vacation Bible School; Discipleship Ministry; and the C.A.R. Resource Center. Minister Heggs is currently enrolled as a senior at the John Leland Center for Theological Studies in Arlington, Virginia.

Minister Heggs is a native Arlingtonian who attended the then-segregated Charles H. Drew Elementary School during the 1960s. Minister Heggs matriculated through the Arlington County Public School System to graduate from Wakefield Senior High School in 1976. Minister Heggs is employed by the Arlington County Fire Department as an executive assistant to the fire chief. She is the proud, single parent of one son, Arien Heggs. Minister Heggs attributes her spiritual upbringing to her father, widower Dea Tom P. Heggs of Arlington, Virginia, who has been continually serving in ministry at the St. John Baptist Church in Alexandria, Virginia, for over fifty years.

To testify of God's continuing manifested glory in her life, the revelation of Romans 8:28 declares: "And we know that all things work together for the good to them that love God, to them who are the called according to his purpose." (Source: Minister Tonia Heggs)

Minister Dejohn Campbell

Minister Dejohn Campbell currently serves as an associate minister and in the youth ministry at Macedonia Baptist Church in Arlington, Virginia. Minister Campbell is a native of Arlington, Virginia. He has executive produced two, web-based talk shows, has been an interviewer for AVN's *Arlington Stories*, co-host for Arlington County's 19th Annual Feel the Heritage Festival, and selected as a finalist for international IT Firm SAIC's Patriotic Song Writing Competition for his original song, "Our Heroes."

In addition to being a college student, Campbell became one of the youngest producers for one of the most successful T.V. and film production companies in Washington, D.C., and currently is employed by a property management company in Falls Church, Virginia. In addition, he has sat on the Bonder and Amanda Johnson Board and currently sits on the board for Winters Lane Productions, Dominion Stage, and Jireh's Place. Campbell is a former student of Drew Model Elementary, Kenmore Middle, and Wakefield High Schools. Being a part of the Arlington Public Schools has helped him to become the man he is today, and his tenure as a student in APS will never be forgotten.

Campbell's family being a part of the Nauck community has stretched all the way back to his great-grandparents, as they have lived in the Nauck community for over fifty years. In addition to his great-grandparents being a part of the Nauck community, his mother, aunts, uncles, and a host of his cousins have attended Arlington Public Schools and have been a part of the Nauck community. Whether it's attending Wakefield, visiting "docs," or attending services at Macedonia, Campbell and his family love the Nauck community. Campbell lives by the quote, "The purpose of life is to live a life of purpose." (Source: Minister Dejohn Campbell)

Reverend Morris Gregory Williams

Reverend Morris Gregory Williams was born on February 22, 1954, in Washington, D.C. He is the third son and last child born to Reverend Ely Williams and Deaconess Estelle Williams-Williamson. Along with his two-older brothers, Reverend Ronald and Ricky, Greg was raised in Arlington, Virginia, and attended Arlington County Schools. In 1971 Greg enlisted in the United States Army, where he served as a field artilleryman in Fort Sill, Oklahoma, and in Giessen, Germany. In January 1972, Greg was honorably discharged from the U.S. Army. After attending Howard University, he became a stockbroker and, for over the eighteen years, he worked at several NYSE listed brokerage firms on Wall Street, NYC.

In 1996 he surrendered to the calling from God and began studying and preparing for the Ministry. He was licensed to preach the Gospel in December 1998 at the Macedonia Baptist Church. He began his Seminary training at the Samuel DeWitt School of Theology at Virginia Union University, where he graduated with a Masters of Divinity in May 2004. He began serving God under the leadership of Dr. Leonard Hamlin, Pastor of the Macedonia Baptist Church. Reverend Williams has also served as Chaplain at several hospitals in the area. He has also served as Chaplain in the North Carolina and Virginia Prison systems. Reverend Williams was ordained at the Macedonia Baptist Church in October 2006 and is currently serving at the Mt. Olive Baptist Church in Partlow, Virginia.

Reverend Williams was married to Blanch Harps on February 6, 1982. Out of this union, three children, Henri, Christen, and Gregory, were born. He has three grandchildren, and his fourth grandchild is expected in October 2013. (Resource: Reverend Morris Gregory Williams)

Minister-in-Training Cheryl Henderson

M.I.T. Cheryl Henderson was born and raised in Northern Virginia. She moved to Arlington, Virginia, in 1964 with her parents and siblings. In October 1968, she gave her life to Christ and became a member of Macedonia Baptist Church. During her membership at Macedonia, she became a member of the Gospel chorus, UIW Choir, Coordinator of the Hospitality Ministry, and a walker for Christ Team Captain. Growing up Cheryl was a member of the Bells of Joy. After graduating from Discipleship Classes, she became a discipleship class facilitator.

Cheryl and her husband, Stanley Henderson, reside in Dale City, Virginia. They have two daughters, Jolanda Parson and Stacie Henderson, one son, Jerome Davis (deceased), a son-in-law, Chez Parson, and four grandchildren.

Cheryl received her calling to preach while attending discipleship classes at Macedonia Baptist Church. Currently Cheryl is attending the Lighthouse Bible Institute of Maryland.

One of her favorite Bible verses is Deuteronomy 6:5: "And thou shalt love the Lord thy God with all thine heart, and with all thy soul, and with all thy might." (Source: Minister-in-Training Cheryl Henderson)

Reverend Ernie Tyrone Moore

Reverend Ernie Tyrone More was born June 4, 1947, in Freedmen's Hospital to the late George Henry and Johnnie Coleman Moore. Ernie is the fourth child of three brothers and three sisters. He was educated in the Arlington County Public School System, attending Drew Elementary, Hoffman-Boston Junior-Senior High School, and graduating in 1966 from Wakefield High School. After graduation he enlisted in the United States Air Force. He attended basic training at Lackland Air Force Base in San Antonio, Texas and technical training school at Shepard Air Force Base in Wichita Falls, Texas. His assignments included tours of duty at George Air Force Base in California; Southeast Asia; and Edwards Air Force Base in California. He received an honorable discharge on January 17, 1973.

After discharge he became a law enforcement officer, serving seven years with the Federal Protective Service, District II, Zone V. In 1981 he transferred to a white-collar civil service position as a security specialist, where he was employed with the Office of the Chief of Staff Army, U.S. Army Intelligence Agency and retired on March 28, 1997 after thirty years, six months, and seventeen days of service.

In 1998 he answered the call to ministry, completing studies at the Lomax Bible Institute, and receiving his Diploma in Biblical Studies. In 2003 he graduated suma cum laude with a Bachelor's in Christian Ministry from Chesapeake Bible

College and Seminary. In 2006 he received a Master of Ministry from Chesapeake Bible College and Seminary. He presently serves as an associate minister at Lomax A.M.E. Zion Church.

Reverend Moore is married to Donna Michelle Anderson Moore. They have two children, Marcia Lanier Hinton and Erica Tonya Moore, and two grandchildren, Monica Lanier Hinton and Makiya Lanier Hinton. (Source: Reverend Ernie Moore)

Minister Hazel Garner-Duckett

Minister Hazel Garner-Duckett, known to most by the name of Retta, was born and raised in Arlington County. She is a lifelong member of Macedonia Baptist Church; she was baptized at the age of five and rededicated her life through baptism after accepting her call into the Ministry. She was licensed to preach the Gospel on July 30, 2008.

Hazel has been married to Walton B. Duckett for fourteen years. With this union there are two sons, Willie Jamil Garner, twenty-four, who has a degree in musical theatre from Shenandoah University and is now employed with Arlington County Public Schools, and Marcel B. Duckett, twenty-two, who graduated high school from Lackey in Maryland, attended Bowie State University, and is now the assistant manager at CVS in Maryland.

Hazel graduated from Wakefield High School and has continued her education by attending general classes at Northern Virginia Community College. Most recently she has completed the bachelor's and master's program at Chesapeake University (Lomax Campus), with a Certificate of Completion in Biblical Studies.

Hazel, who has a personal passion for writing, has over forty years in administrative work. For the last sixteen years, she has been employed in the Arlington & Alexandria School Systems as an administrative assistant. Her employment has proven to be more rewarding than she had expected. It has afforded her the opportunity to share, love, be an example, and witness the love of God to those children and young adults who just may not have an ear or this example in their life. During her employment with the school systems, Hazel has taken several courses, including Letter Writing for Secretaries, Positive Relationships with Colleagues, Time Management and other Stress Reducers, Supporting School Programs, Empowering Support Staff to make a Difference, Conflict Resolution/Before It Gets Out of Hand, and Strategies that Work, to help her learn the fundamentals of teaching comprehension for understanding and engagement.

As a member of Macedonia, Hazel has worked as an assistant to the Superintendent of Sunday school and has been active in many ministries, such as the Bells of Joy, MBC Ensemble (formerly the YPC's), June Calendar Club, Pastor's Aid Club, Missionary Society, Prison Ministry, Vacation Bible School Teacher, Discipleship Class Instructor, Prayer Ministry, Unity in Worship, and Adult Praise Team.

Hazel believes that worship is as essential to your walk as oxygen is to your physical survival. If your worship life, which incorporates prayer, praise and study, is not a part of who you are and what you do on a daily basis, then it is impossible to please God and develop a relationship with Him. There are two favorite scriptures that she often stands on as reference in her walk with the Lord. Proverbs 3:5: "Trust in the Lord with all your heart and lean not to your own understanding, but in all your ways acknowledge him and he shall direct your paths." I Corinthians 10-13: "No temptation has overtaken you except such as is common to man, but God is faithful, who will not allow you to be tempted beyond what you able, but with the temptation will also make the way of escape, that you may be able to bear it."

Hazel is a disciple of the Lord and seeks to follow the path that He has set for her, realizing that her life has been purposed to serve Him and be fishers of men for the building up of His and the edifying of His word. (Source: Minister Hazel Garner-Duckett)

Biography

Alfred O. Taylor, Jr., was born on July 28, 1934, in Arlington County, Virginia (Nauck). He attended the Arlington County Public Schools until completion of the third grade, after which his parents, products of the D.C. Public School System, transferred him to the Stevens Elementary School in Washington, D.C. After completing Stevens, he attended Francis Junior High School and the Armstrong Technical High School, graduating from both schools with honors. He completed his undergraduate education at the Washington Technical Institute with a B.S. in Technical Teacher Training (Vocational Education), an M.A. in Administration and Supervision of Adult Education from Federal City College, and his Ed.D. from the Virginia Polytechnic Institute and State University in Administration of Higher Education. His love for education, especially vocational/technical, has allowed him to pursue additional classes at the Rochester Institute of Technology, University of Pittsburgh, University of California at Berkeley, and others.

After high school, he pursued his love of printing in the private and public sectors, where he held supervisory and management positions in both. During this time, he was also part owner of two printing establishments, Our Printers in Washington, D.C., and the Quality Printing Company in Capitol Heights, Maryland.

In 1969 he left the United States Government Printing Office to further develop the Printing and Publishing Program at the newly created Washington Technical Institute, where he served as professor, coordinator, and Department chairperson. In 1979 after the establishment of the University of the District of Columbia, he was appointed the Associate Dean of the College of Physical Science, Engineering, and Technology. During his tenure in this position, he was detailed to serve as the Coordinator of Admissions and Records (three years) and Assistant Provost for Student Services (three years). He was later appointed the Assistant Dean for the College of Professional Studies and served in that position until being named the Acting Dean in 1997. During his tenure at UDC, he also had the privilege to teach in Nairobi, Kenya. He retired from the University in 1999 after thirty-one years of service. The University honored him as the recipient of the Ronald H. Brown Leadership Award at their 2014 Founder's Day Celebration.

He is still active in his community, serving as President of the Nauck Civic Association; Chairman of the Juvenile Detention Commission for Northern Virginia; member of the Board of Directors of the Bonder and Amanda Johnson Community Development Corporation; member of the Board of Directors of the Nauck Revitalization Organization; member of the Board of Directors of the Alliance for Housing Solutions; member of the advisory committee for Arlington Career Center; member of the Arlington Police Chief's Advisory Committee, Joint GMU/Arlington County Advisory Board; past President and Executive Board Member of the Arlington Branch of the NAACP; past Chairperson of the Arlington County Local Human Rights Committee; member of the Board of Directors of the Northern Virginia Health Systems Agency; member of the Board of Directors of OAR; and past Basileus of the Omega Psi Phi Fraternity, Inc.

He is also active in the religious community, where he serves and holds many offices, including: Chairman of the Deacon's Ministry at the Macedonia Baptist Church and past Chairman of the Board of Trustees of the Maple Springs Baptist Bible College and Seminary, to name a few. He was a substitute teacher with the Arlington County Public School System after his retirement from UDC.

The driving factors behind his lifelong service are his parents, who were always active in the community. His father was Arlington's Assistant Superintendent of the Sanitation Division, retiring after forty-four years of service. His mother retired from the federal government as a Supervisor of Data Processing at the Naval Research Laboratory and was also instrumental in helping the Veterans Memorial YMCA purchase the ground and construction of its building.

His biggest personal joy is seeing the Nauck community as a viable link to the history, growth, and success of Arlington. Having the Nauck community seated at the table in planning its future is exactly what he's been working on for years, and he is not stopping, He's still challenged that not enough Nauck residents are convinced that they do have a voice in the growth and direction of their neighborhood. He also wants to better assimilate the different ethnic groups into the spirit and fabric of the community.

He has been married to Delores Smith Taylor, a retired D.C. Public School teacher, for sixty-one years. They have been blessed with two children: Kenneth, gospel music artist, publicist, and CEO of Teemade Productions, and Karen, a special education para-professional at Gunston Middle School. They are also blessed with three grandsons, Kourtnay, Aaron, and Ariel, as well as two great granddaughters, Miya and Maliah.